97-300

£1·00

A FENMAN IN AFRICA

I

The author standing near a baobab tree, Zambesi Valley 1981

II

A FENMAN IN AFRICA

or

A letter from Rhodesia

The author's diary of a stay on a Rhodesian Farm
and a hunting camp in the African bush.
with related correspondence .

PHIL GRAY

Reedbush Press 2006

First published by Reedbush Press, Cambridgeshire
2006

© Phil Gray 2006

ISBN 0-9541994-1-3

Other books by the same author
The Washlanders
Fenland Fowler

This book is dedicated to Anne

Printed in Great Britain by
PrintOnDemand-Worldwide.com

Contents

Acknowledgements

My thanks to my dear friend Corona Thornycroft who kindly gave permission for me to write this book, for the use of letters received from her and her late husband Nigel spanning thirty years and for the loan of personal papers photographs and Game Books.

Foreword

The Zambesi Valley is one of the world's last great wilderness areas. A bushveldt of dense hot scrub, massive baobab trees, giant anthills and riverside cliffs bored with the nests of thousands of bee-eaters. It is home to a fantastic variety of wildlife, big game and small - and the birds. I was immensely lucky and privileged to be invited to join a hunting and fishing camp in the valley in 1981.

This book tells the story of that camp and how this fenman came to be involved due to a chance purchase of a book written by a POW while he was an unwilling "guest" of the Gestapo. There are extracts from letters written during Rhodesia's own troubles and subsequent letters describing exciting moments from other camps in the bush.

I hope that the reader will get the feel of the hunter's camp in the bush where no tourist's foot pollutes the dust. Of sleeping in the open with a large fire to keep the hyenas away, lying listening to the exciting night noises and waking to the cry of the fish eagle. Then above all, the ever present thrill of the mix of wild beauty with the hint of danger, the savageness and tranquillity, which is the Zambesi Valley.

Phil Gray
Whittlesey

Cambridgeshire

1

A meeting of like minds?

When I bought the book from Elderkin's Gunmakers Shop in Spalding, Lincolnshire I little realised what would result from that innocent purchase. It was 1959 and I was just 18 years of age. Elderkin's shop at that time held a certain magic for the young shooting enthusiast – stuffed pheasants and mallard in lifelike flying postures were suspended on almost invisible wires from the ceiling and so appeared to be whizzing over ones head. Sporting prints and manufacturers mounted displays of various types of cartridges filled any available space on the walls. I had gone there with a friend who had taken his gun in for a minor repair and while he was engrossed in his business I strolled from room to room to see what took my fancy from the shops large stock of guns. Whilst browsing through the rows of gleaming barrels my eye was attracted to a shelf of books. Among these volumes was blue-jacketed book entitled *Fowlers Moon*. I can rarely resist a book once it has taken my interest and so it wasn't long before this copy became mine.

It told of a young mans first season at coastal wildfowling on the salt marshes of the Wash. The book was even better than I expected and I read it from cover to cover at one sitting. Perhaps it had added interest for me because, although the author had taken pains to disguise the locations and scenes of his expeditions, they were familiar to me and I was sure I could identify them. Over the next few years I annually re-read the book and each time came to thinking. "I'll bet that was at Terrington Marsh, or the fair he mentions must have been Lynn Mart!" In the end I decided that I must try to contact the author, one Nigel Thornycroft and ask him to put me out of my misery. The publishers had lost contact and the only address available was that at the bottom of the preface. It merely read Merryhill, Marandellas, Southern Rhodesia. Not much to go on, but hang it all, I had nothing to lose by trying. I wrote to Mr Thornycroft at the address assuring him that as all the coastal shooting was now leased to wildfowling clubs he would not be causing any damage by confirming or rejecting my speculations. As it was several years since the book had been published and I had no idea whether or not the author was still at the same address I have to say that I was more than surprised and not a little delighted when, after a couple of months, a letter bearing Rhodesian stamps and postmark dropped through my letterbox. It read:

Merryhill
10th August 1972

Dear Mr Gray
Your letter of August 2nd gave me infinite pleasure and also stirred many happy memories of pre-war days.

You're quite right of course, it all centred round your bit of coast, in fact there are probably very few creeks between Snettisham and Boston I haven't stumbled into at one time or another. I first "discovered" the area from Cambridge in '28 and used to spend far too much of my winters down there for my tutor's entire approval. The Welney Washes were another v. happy hunting ground of mine. And I knew most of the old plover netters and shepherds. In fact I was so bitten with wildfowling in general that I was determined to live in the area and so started up a small silver fox farm near a village called Blackborough End between Lynn and Swaffham. For the ten years before the war spent most of my moons, dawns and dusks on the coast and most of the daytime shooting inland! The war and rationing of course, put paid to that. I was with the Norfolk Regiment and put in the bag at St. Valarie in 1940 and virtually

2

haven't been down to the Wash since – though have had a few trips to the N. Solway coast in '46 and '47.

It seems strange to me to imagine all the coastal area controlled by various wildfowlers associations, but it is I imagine, a very sound move towards conservation; even in my day I used to get pretty livid some weekends the way some of the "furriners" would loose off at almost any goose in sight. In fact I was probably pretty lucky not to have been bumped the only time I have been back to UK – in January 1954 when I left Salisbury, Rhodesia at 10 am one day and by midnight the following night was out on the Solway flats under a full moon where I spent most of the next fortnight in happy ignorance (*that he was in a no-shooting zone*) and also collected 13 geese.

You aren't far out in your guesses at the various scenes I described. That wigeon flight was on the Snettisham side of Lynn, Wootton Marsh in fact and Lynn Mart <u>was</u> the cause of it – it was in fact, the only time I ever came across wigeon in any quantity that side. Perhaps the flashes (*shallow pools left by receding high tides*) where I had most success were those about a mile South of the Nene Lighthouses. Peter Scott and I had one terrific flight of 46 there. Another very useful couple of flashes were in the angle of the sea wall out from the old windmill near Admiralty Point – and I had one memorable night only a mile or or so North of the old Coastguard Station at Terrington. Blank days of course, were legion. I never did much good with wigeon North of the Nene, though used to get a fair few geese at times between there and "Shep Whites". I say a fair few – which sounds v. grand. In fact my annual total of geese ran between a dozen and twenty, as I never would go after them inland. Five was my record – one morning of dense fog when the gods were kind just off Admiralty Point and I probably averaged 60 –100 flights – dawn, dusk and moon – a year.

Probably the worst thing about that book was how it came to be written. I'd often scribbled odd articles for the "Field" and such but never contemplated a book. In fact, it probably saved my reason as in the summer of '43 I was picked up by the Gestapo on the Swiss border having travelled across

3

half Germany on foot by night during the previous fortnight. Was slammed into an underground cell in Ulm prison where I spent the next three months without seeing the sun and came out more or less horizontal, weighing less than 9 stone. (*Nigel was well over six feet tall*) Anyway, I had in my pocket the tail end of a roll of bronco (*toilet roll*) and a stub of pencil and most of the book was written in minute script on both sides of the bronco with a v. keen eye on the spy hole in the door! It never was discovered – but took a lot of deciphering afterwards. I am surprised it is still available – I tidied it up here and sent it over to UK for publication and that's almost the last I thought of it. It also kept my wife happy doing the illustrations, which are rather fun. She was a Norfolk girl and used to do quite a bit of mud-larking with me.

Are there any big guns left on the Wash these days? I went out punting several times pre-war with Peter Scott from the Nene Lighthouses. Fascinating. If at times nerve racking days – and some of the best were bloodless – as with most 'fowling.

Post-war we blued our "blood money" in having a look round various parts of the world with a view to settling as it looked impossible to us, to bring up a family in the country in England. Finally we pitched up here, acquired a couple of thousand acres of virgin Africa and have tried to beat it into a home. It's been a wonderful struggle. There's no Social Security. You stand or fall by your own efforts and most of what you can't build or make you do without. It's a dawn to dusk life, with your paper work to follow. Country-wise, it can't touch England, Nowhere I have ever been to my mind can; but real country life in England today is a shrinking commodity and we now have some 6000 acres to play with. A neighbour went bust three or four years ago due to sanctions and we took a big gulp and bought him out. We now have enough land to own cattle as well as grow crops – tobacco and maize. We're desperately hard up; most Rhodesian farmers are today owing to the sanctions war. But we're here to stay and are bound to win in the end, as we can't afford to lose. One does fight for ones home you know. The sad part of this battle is that it's against our own folk – your politicians anyway. Commerce, industry, and trade in general are flourishing, buildings going up everywhere. And the hard fact remains that this is by far the most peaceful and happy part of Africa. South Africa somehow misses it, there's tension there and the "liberated" states North of the Zambesi are pure shambles. However you don't want these kinds of opinions.

Shooting-wise Rhodesia has nothing wonderful to offer. Some of the francolin are fun. Guinea fowl are the main shooting bird. They can put a cock pheasant to shame on the ground and are no-ones fools to outwit. In the air – just guinea fowl and on the table a vehicle for good cooking. Our duck are tame compared to the Northern hemisphere ones. Red-billed teal, Pochard (S.A. variety), knob-nose, black nun duck and odd specimens of various species – I have shot both gargany and cape wigeon – though neither of them "should" have been here. White faced duck – floppy little brutes, but quite attractive and are on the increase, pygmy geese and white backs. Thing is this country is changing environmentally – especially as regards water – so quickly it's hardly true and is very exciting. On this farm for instance, I've built twenty-three dams in the past twenty years – varying from ½ an acre to 180 acres – and this is fairly normal and must and does affect bird life. I had three pairs of teal and pochard nest with me this year – also two pairs of black duck and this in an area, which held no water twenty years ago. It really is a rather fascinating country – there's so much to do if you don't mind rolling your sleeves up and getting on with it. And I do believe we are handling the race problem better than anywhere in the world today – far better than UK or America from all reports. But again, I'm wandering from things of interest –

We have some good fishing – most dams are stocked with black bass and various tilapia species. I've done all mine and there's some of the best trout fishing I've ever had in the Eastern mountains and some v. lovely streams. Tiger fish can be exciting though not that much more edible than a pike, and with v. similar bones.

I've managed to get off on a fortnights big game hunting most years and that can be an exciting pastime – sleeping on the ground, all manner of night noises. I'm off down the Zambesi Valley tail end of this month. Four of us have a concession over about 1000 square miles for a fortnight and are allowed – if we can come up with them – 8 buffalo, and 2 elephant and a certain amount of smaller stuff to keep the pot boiling. No white dwelling within 100 miles. One takes all ones own bedding a couple of trucks and jeeps and lives off the bush. Half a dozen Africans to cut up and dry any meat – it's v. much a point of honour that no meat is to be wasted. I've only once known any on any of our trips – a bull elephant who fell on its back in a narrow crevasse and we couldn't cut through to the side before it went bad...

It's an intriguing game you and a single tracker are out pre-dawn, trying to cut back where the beast you are after has come down to drink at night – then on the track for maybe 4-6 hours and 8 – 12 miles, if you can hold to it – then, more often than not a wild crashing stampede as the buff you're after gets your wind – and a long trek back to camp. Or, you may get your shot – usually between 15 to 30 yards, as the cover is thick - and you have to cut a jeep road in, windlass the body up and back to camp in rather greater triumph.

I'm drooling on at an unconscionable length – happens I'd a blank evening ahead when your letter arrived and its now 8.30 and time for bed – with a 5.30 am kick off ahead.

Do, if you can spare the time, write again and give me the current wildfowling picture – it was so very much my life and is perhaps the thing I miss the most. Better still, come out and see this country for yourself!

With warmest regards

Yours sincerely

Nigel Thornycroft

So began a correspondence that was to last for 16 years. My own letters keeping Nigel abreast of the wildfowling scene in general and my little adventures in particular, while his told of life on the farm and of the wildlife and duck flighting on the dams. What where the dams? I wondered. Must be artificial lakes of sorts. Now and again he described the annual hunting trip to the Zambesi valley and the big game and fish they encountered. Nigel's descriptive writing was so good that one could almost picture the scene as they got in close to elephant or stalked Kudu. When our first contact was made however, Rhodesia was in the middle of its quarrel with our British Labour Government who, in their haste to "free" those countries remaining in the British Empire, seemed to be taking the side of the communist inspired native political groups. Sanctions and terrorist raids were making life difficult. The early letters I received are now probably minor historical documents and a few selected fragments may give an insight into the conditions and attitudes of the time. The first was dated 15th March 1975 and after telling me about the various wildlife he had seen on the farm and of how the crops were faring we come in where Nigel is talking about the tobacco harvest.

… I have actually started grading some of the earliest curings and got 9000 lbs away last week. Sales start 23rd so we will then know a bit how it is likely to sell this year. I hope it will be higher than last year, but its all got to be exported and sanction dodging isn't cheap! It's going to make very amusing reading when all this nonsense is over – but meanwhile doesn't exactly grease the wheels of progress. You're quite right in your surmise that that your news media exaggerate affairs out here out of all proportion and much of what they print is a completely baseless tissue of lies from reports that filter back here. The fact is that Rhodesia today, except round the fringes is probably as peaceful, happy and law abiding a country as any in the world. There are a1000 or so terrorists in and around our borders. Russian armed, trained and indoctrinated making tip and run dashes into the country, burning, raping and looting. With the wild country, largely uninhabited and the long border, it is impractical to stop them crossing and this does make life uncomfortable in the border areas. But I'm utterly confident that we can cope very effectively with anything the black states, even with Russian and Chinese arms and training can throw against us. Moreover, its nonsense to talk of racist war and racist oppression. Our fighting forces are in the proportion of 2-1 black – white and our police force an even higher ratio. And they are first class at their job. Moreover, the vast majority of the black population are contented. Nkomo and Co represent a very small proportion. Personally I can't see very much coming out of the current series of talks. None whatsoever of black majority rule in the foreseeable future. Starvation today is rife in almost all of the "free" black states. Mozambique in particular – there'll be a revolt there shortly over Machel – With black rule Rhodesia would rapidly become another such black slum. Even today, despite sanctions it is keeping a lot of Africa alive food-wise and sheer hunger will open even more doors, which (Harold) Wilson and his kidney are trying rather hopelessly to keep closed to make good his boast to crush us. To be honest I don't think we could cope with a full-scale armoured Russian manned invasion – not on our own. Though even that wouldn't be an Angola style walk-through and there would be several bloodied noses around. But I can't see this happening just yet a while and I firmly believe that the world is slowly coming to its senses and seeing what tools they're being made of in their relations towards Africa. All we want is more honest open – minded folk to come and see for themselves and form opinions from knowledge and not from the emotive bleatings of students and mischievous and probably communist inspired propaganda. Damn, I'm sorry – this letter has deteriorated into a political diatribe – will try to do better next time!!

      Just every good wish to you both
      Nigel

Parts of that letter prophesised what actually happened nearly thirty years later when Zimbabwe was ruined by its own government. Before inserting any more letters however and more to keep things in some sort of chronological order this might be the place to tell of our first face-to-face meeting. Nigel had said that he was coming over to England for the first time since 1954 to visit his brother in Shropshire and would like to meet me if I was free. Naturally I left him in no doubt that he was more than welcome, so arrangements were made and he duly pitched up on our doorstep at the end of November 1975.

I had advised him to bring some suitable gear for wildfowling and thus equipped on the Friday we set off for Admiralty Point on Terrington Marsh on the Norfolk coast of the Wash. After parking the van, donning our thigh boots and weatherproof clothing we shouldered our guns and strode off along the sea wall for a "memory trip" before the evening – cum moon flight.

I had wanted my guest to see his old stamping ground in daylight so we had driven over soon after lunch. Except for a new enclosure of reclaimed land he said the place had not changed a great deal. My dog at that time was old and infirm finding the rough terrain of the marsh heavy going. As this was more of a visit than a serious shooting day I had left him at home and missed him almost at once. At a bend in the bank we encountered three duck on a nearby creek. Nigel hid behind a mud bank while I did a detour to bring me behind the birds. I achieved the first part of my goal but not the second, which was to drive the birds over my friend. When I showed myself the duck jumped of course, but incredibly flew back past me. They were the other side of a wide and full creek where I couldn't retrieve so I did not shoot at them even though they were in easy shot. We laughed at being so neatly outwitted and walked on along the sea wall.

Just off a certain corner we inspected the shallow pools in the marsh known as flashes. These were full after the earlier high tide and there was definitely evidence of recently feeding wild duck, particularly wigeon. We could see brent geese grazing a few hundred yards further on so put them up for my visitor's benefit. He said that in his day, before the war, brent were rare on this part of the coast and if they saw half a dozen it was something to remember. What a glorious sight and sound this 500 offered as they jumped and flew off low over the saltings.

We did not expect to see much at dusk as the moon was due to rise around 7.30 pm but as we were on the spot anyway, we split up to try our luck. In the last of the light I saw three teal buzz past low and very fast. Too fast for me to even think about raising the gun. Before long there came the bump of a single shot from where Nigel was hiding a quarter of a mile away. Moments later a dull thump told that he had scored. When he re-joined me he told me that he'd collected a young cock wigeon. "He was an outrider to a team of seven and with all that marsh to fly over, a damned unlucky bird."

Jumping muddy gutters and brushing through the stiff marsh grasses we eventually got back to the sea wall were we lay and ate sandwiches and pork pie while we waited to see what the moon was going to bring. After an hour or so spent talking of marshland experiences the sky was clear and bright with no sign of the necessary light clouds. We decided to drive back to my local fresh marshes known as Whittlesey Wash and hope that cloud would drift up while we were travelling. Three quarters of an hour later we were there, but obliging clouds there were not. Undaunted we split up along the edge of a large stretch of floodwater. We heard mallard and then an, at that time, unusual sound at Whittlesey, canada geese. The latter came, unseen over our water and seemed to go on over the nearby river. Cloud refused to appear so in the end we had to call it a night and as we moved off a pair of canadas rose from the far end of the water. Bright as it was we still could not see them. The same brightness gave us an easy walk back to the van as is was very light and our shadows danced along drove ahead of us. We crammed a lot into that weekend, tramping round the Washlands where Nigel added three snipe to his bag and long sessions over a glass or two hearing about Rhodesia, the farm and the hunts in the bush. While we were thus engrossed I brought out my copy of *Fowler's Moon* to be signed by the author who kindly obliged and adding – *"For Phil, who has just shown me that through all the changes over the past few decades, the spirit and joy of wildfowling is as live and keen as ever it was."*

By the following year exaggerated press reports in the UK and other parts of the world on the parlous plight of their country and how sanctions were having a serious affect inspired Ian Smith's Rhodesian Government to print a message on aerogrammes for people to send to concerned relatives. The message took up about half the usual writing space but put over their side of the story. A little bit of counter – propaganda perhaps. Out of historical interest I reproduce one on the next page.

16 Apr 76

Dear Phil — I thought this might amuse you

No doubt you are worried about the situation in Rhodesia, particularly in view of all the sensational headlines and horrific articles which appear in the Press. The psychological war being waged against Rhodesia through many of the news media of the world has escalated to such proportions of misrepresentation that many observers outside this country find it difficult to separate fact from fiction.

Daily examples of deliberate distortions and half truths are carried in the headlines of the world's newspapers and radio and television networks. The initial feelings of unease which assailed the people of Rhodesia and their friends abroad have now turned to anger at the perpetrators of these attempts to undermine the morale of our country and its supporters.

Scores of journalists from all over the world have descended upon Rhodesia and, believe it or not, are hard put to find enough to do or see. There are no massacres and bloodbaths, there are no massive terrorist force build-ups, there is no panic or hysteria, and there are no queues of people leaving the country. Many of the photographs and Press reports which have been sent to us by our friends bear no relationship whatever to the real situation in Rhodesia. In fact, some of the photographs and film were not even taken in Rhodesia!

Instead, these journalists find themselves in a country where they can travel safely with no fears of bomb explosions. They can walk through the cities at night with no fear of being mugged. They can spend a day in the country and watch the soil being tilled and the crops gathered. They can go to restaurants or a nightclub and pay less for better food than in many other countries in the world and they do not find sandbags or steel shutters over the windows of their chosen venue, nor are they searched before entering.

They find black and white Rhodesians mingling peacefully together and carrying on with their day to day jobs as they have done for many years. They find that there are sporting events, theatres, cinemas, horse racing and many other facets of entertainment available to them as they would elsewhere. They do see troops coming and going from their barracks, because there is an anti-terrorist war being waged on our borders, and there are shortages — of things like razor blades, black pepper, light bulbs and the more exotic foods and toiletries.

And, some are disappointed, because every journalist lives on the hopes of scooping a disaster. And so, stories are made up — and elaborated upon to make them more sensational at editorial desks thousands of miles away. What much of the world Press does not wish to print are the true facts about Rhodesia. That she has weathered the last 10 years so well, in terms of internal peace, productivity, growth and racial harmony, despite the effects of boycotts and sanctions.

We do not deny that Rhodesians are going through difficult times — difficult but not drastic, and compared with most countries in the world today Rhodesians have much to be thankful for.

This is a completely true & factual account of affairs here to day, we have had it printed to send to friends as we are becoming rather bored with the horror tales

12

In 1978 things were warming up with the war getting closer to home as the following letter indicates.

Marandellas
7ᵗʰ August 1978

Dear Phil
        I'm due and overdue to drop you a line I fear me – and this is not a very inspiring effort. But we are going through a pretty tricky period at the present and quite apart from straight farming the terrorist problem is a very real one. Quite apart from attacks on white homesteads – we've had four on neighbours this past month during two of which we could actually hear the heavy stuff going off, they've developed a possibly even more worrying technique recently, of attacking and burning farm compounds (where the African workers live) with odd murders and mutilations – castrating males, cutting lips off women – which of course drives all the labour into the high hills. I may say that these animals are followers of one Robert Mugabe. All these terrs are armed with automatic rifles, grenades, rockets, mortars and mines and are Russian/Cuban trained.
    In this district we're forming our own fighting guard force and follow up units and just about every man, woman and child is involved quite apart from army and police. Cattle rustling – all tied up with terr activity – this district has lost well over the 1000 head butchered and stolen in the last eight weeks – is another nuisance and all the ensuing follow ups, ambushes and what have you, mean thousands of hours lost. Right, we've killed a few – it all sounds so simple till you see the thousands of square miles of rugged country they have to hide up in. And these chaps are fit and can easily cover thirty miles in a night. We're not beaten yet, by a long chalk, but we're all living under a bit of a strain as you may imagine. Not much time for leisure and a lot of farmers have been driven out. With sanctions on top, which though one laughs at them have in fact cut most farm

13

incomes to subsistence or debt. The next few months may well be a bit dicey and I shall think of you with some envy when I'm spending a nice moonlight night lying up in the bush in some rocky crevice in ambush and how under that same moon you may be hearing the geese jump and the wigeon calling. At least I'll probably be warmer!...

And this next letter tells how they persisted in trying to work a few days fishing into the heavy schedule and what a risky business it was.

Marandellas
14th May 1979

Dear Phil,
I have been wondering quite a lot what the past winter brought you in the way of 'fowl. From all accounts it may have been a dead loss and too hard? Or you may have come in for the magic of the thaw and the returning legions. I can remember one early winter on the Wash when the cold went on and on and the saltings were lifeless for weeks – and the thaw came all unexpected right at the end of the season....

He then moves on to politics and the faint hope that the newly elected Thatcher Government might come to the aid of its beleaguered ex-pats.

...As sadly we are being pressed very hard at the moment, both economically and physically. We are literally fighting a fairly bloody war with one hand and in one space of time trying to keep going a fairly man-sized job with the other. You can imagine a one man business – or farm - when the one man has to be actively fighting on average 90 days a year and subject to local emergency call ups at 5 minutes notice day or night for local defence and farm attacks by terrs. And with the partial breakdown of control one of our major troubles locally is looting and theft by the youthful element. Our area alone has lost 3600 head of cattle! Hard to picture in a country like England. We are in fact, holding fairly well, but many folk are getting exhausted – and very bitter with the outside world.

Don't let me sound too gloomy. I, and most of my neighbours hereabouts are by no means finished yet, its just rather boring that ones amusements are cut down so drastically! No hunting – I'm getting too old anyway, but I would like to have introduced some of my young to the thrills I've had myself and perhaps hand over a little knowledge.

We had a sad weekend just passed, which has probably contributed to my current outlook. I've told you about that very lovely stretch of trout water we have on the Mozambique border. Well, with an awful lot of planning and scheming we'd at last managed to inveigle the army and security forces to allow us in and six of us went up.

We had to camp a couple of miles from the river under army protection. Very well organised – Three mine proofed vehicles, army commissariat; 5 ton truck complete with deep freeze and water bowser. (The army do themselves well!) Rv. A bit late and we got down to the river only by 4.30 pm for a half hours glimpse as we had to be in camp by dusk – 5.30 pm.

River in perfect order and much licking of lips at the thought of the morrow. We did just test our lines and in fact caught 2 fish – 3 and 2 lbs as an appetiser. Next morning, the bird in charge – a Captain in the R.A.R, who also had thoughts of trout, took the 5 ton armoured vehicle down with a patrol of 8 to do a sweep of the valley, as there were reports of a possible terr. base camp in the area. He took one of us out as a shotgun guard for the drive back and left camp at 5.30 am. Expecting him back with the "all clear" around 7.30. Nothing happened and nothing happened. We thought he might have got into some local engagement and he doing a follow up where we would be a nuisance, but at 9.30 two of us set out in one of the Land Rovers to investigate and met three very blackened and bruised and rather gory bodies limping back.

What had happened was the heavy had hit a landmine – a very nasty reinforced one – on the road. Mercifully, just after he'd unloaded his troops to do the patrol and turned round to fetch us. The three in the vehicle had been blown out and most of their clothes ripped off by the blast. The vehicle lifted off the road and pretty shattered. The mine proofing had in fact, saved their lives, though the one member of our party was immobile and we feared a broken back. Mercifully it turned out to be only his jaw and a few ribs. They'd left the patrol on guard and we radioed in for a chopper to fly in to evacuate the casualty. It arrived within a couple of hours and got him out to hospital.

The queer part was that we, within a couple of miles never heard a thing, but the explosion was heard 20 miles away and rattled windows in the hotel where two of the party's wives were staying. But we were really remarkably lucky a) that the 5 ton truck and our 3 Land Rovers had the night before been over that road without detonating the mine and b) that we hadn't gone down in the morning in a Land Rover, which mine proof or not, would have disintegrated with a mine that size. The crater in the road was 4 feet deep and 7 feet across. But a boring end to a much looked forward to fishing trip, and it's going to be damned unlikely that we shall be allowed in at all for some time…

… I'd love to get back to England for another visit this winter, but doubt possibilities unless we see a drastic change here. I still believe there's a chance of this country surviving – if, and only if, enough of us can manage to hang on long enough and keep some sort of finger on the reins. If not it'll follow Zambia and Mozambique and most of the rest of "liberated" Africa into a long dark tunnel of destitution and starvation.

Then comes a paragraph or two on the tobacco harvest after which he ends thus…

You'd laugh at my present situation. An empty house – not mine – dusk just fallen, an FN (*military rifle*) across the arms of a chair alongside, a radio for communication with police HQ a few feet away, also a bottle of beer – not quite so distant. One thing about these guard jobs – you do get time to write the odd letter. Even so, I'd better stop.

Do let me know how the winter treated you.
Very warmest regards to you all,
As ever - Nigel

2
Plans and preparations

It had been freezing hard as we entered the new year of 1980 and as I was on a weeks leave from work I had decided to check the skating prospects on the Whittlesey Wash. The ice on the specially flooded land was good and several other skaters were gliding around. I soon laced up my long bladed Norwegian racing skates and after a few minutes found my ice legs again. As usual old friends were met and we skimmed along together comparing the ice with that of other occasions; hoping it wouldn't snow and spoil the smooth surface; wondering whether or not a match of races would be organised for the weekend - all the usual talk and banter. I had been on the ice for a couple of hours when the son of the local Doctor skated over to me to say that a gentleman and his wife were looking for me. I was surprised and delighted to find Nigel and Corona Thornycroft waiting on the bank. They had come over to spend Christmas with Nigel's brother Guy in Shropshire and then gone on to the Solway Firth after geese. On the way to their friends the Birkbeck's of Westacre in Norfolk they decided to call on the off chance of finding us at home. Luckily my wife Pauline was there and directed them to me while she rustled up some lunch. Back at the house Nigel opened his car boot to reveal a brace of greylag geese that were his bag from the Solway. We spent a happy couple of hours over lunch and not for the first time were Pauline and I invited to go and spend some time on the farm in Rhodesia.

Several months afterwards I had been thinking about the invitation, which had been repeated in subsequent letters and I discussed it with Pauline. She did not want to go and anyway it would have been impractical for us both to be away for so long at the same time. It was decided that if I didn't go soon the opportunity might not arise again. It was difficult to get long periods of leave from my work with the Royal Mail because obviously staff could not all be away at the same time, but with the kind assistance of my boss and generous co-operation of my colleagues it was arranged. I wrote off to Rhodesia to the effect that if the invitation still stood I would like to come. In no time at all the postman handed me the following reply.

Merryhill
4ᵗʰ June '81

Dear Phil

How perfectly splendid – and welcome as the flowers in May. Of <u>course</u> we can put you up. No luxury, but thrice welcome, as and when you can make it and for as long as you care to put up with us. Let us know date and time of arrival and we will meet you at Salisbury airport and thereafter play it by ear.

Now, here is the big excitement, if you can make it. I have a hunting concession from 16ᵗʰ to 25ᵗʰ October in the Zambesi Valley. One of the few <u>really</u> wild spots left. Hunting will be at a discount as it is the very last camp of the year and I've little doubt our quota will have been taken out by then. But the river will be there; the animals will be there. We shall be sleeping under the stars and the night noises will be there and we shall have about 500 square miles to play around in by ourselves - of literally virgin Africa. It'll be as hot as the hobs at that time of year, but a minor penalty. And it really is a chance to see and experience surroundings and a set up which is virtually extinct today. I'll certainly try and see if I can get you in as my guest.

Roughly the set up is this. There is 1000 square miles of Valley the hunters association have on lease from Parks & Wildlife (Government Department). Very strict bag limits of course, which we <u>very</u> strictly abide by. We divide it into two areas and each into a dozen or so 10-day periods for which we draw lots. Price according to bag allowed. (A bull elephant today costs $2400 and we are allowed two for the year!) The last four camps have no official bags, but a chance of leftovers, and they're all I could afford. Anyway I was lucky to get one. Two hunters allowed, but a guest apiece. I'm taking down two sons and a very old friend of mine with whom I've done most of my hunting and probably one of the wisest in big game now alive. I am pretty sure I can squeeze you in as a guest and the river is there to fish in, which is what I'll be doing. Its not luxury living, though I find it utterly fascinating and like the UK coast, the valley has a charm of its own – though terrifying at times. Honestly, if you can make it, say not later than October 10th and stay until at least the end of the month, do. It's an opportunity I've never before been in a position to offer, nor would I to many folk, but you might well appreciate it.

Let me know as soon as possible if you're on and I'll go ahead and see what I can do. You'll have very little expenses. Probably a share in grub and beer and damn all else. We can fit you up with any kit needed but I can't change those dates so do your damndest.

I nearly forgot – your last letter arrived the same mail as mine to you left and gave just as much pleasure as yours always do. No time or space for more – but every good wish.

Nigel

Luckily, October made it easier to arrange at work and I lost no time in confirming the dates with the Thornycrofts. Here are extracts from a flurry of letters which I include because they give an insight into the ups and downs of life in the early 1980's in that part of Africa after their war but when it was still hoped that good sense would prevail.

25th July

Dear Phil

I'm taking the liberty of having a parcel sent to you – a damned awkward one! – in the hopes that you will be able to bring it out to me when you come. It is in fact a trout rod and will come from Ebrall Bros of Shrewsbury. If it's too much of a bore never to worry, I'll give you a forwarding address in Amsterdam. You might, if it does arrive and you can bring it, open the parcel and rub a bit of dirt over the rod in case our Customs are inquisitive! Not that I think they will be but you never know with Afs. I've just, after four months entanglement in red tape, got a parcel worth £6 from their clutches on payment of £11 in "dues" to find that it had been opened and looted of 2 of the 3 packets of fish hooks it contained! So nowadays one looks for alternative routes.

Nigel with a tiger fish from the Zambesi

And then

4ᵗʰ August

...Anyway you're down in my calendar from October 10ᵗʰ –29ᵗʰ and I hope 16ᵗʰ –25ᵗʰ will be in the Valley. There will in fact be little or no hunting left. They've taken tuskless elephant off the quota – I gather someone somewhere along the line made a cock-up and the game department decided that "the herds were being disturbed too much." So, our activity will be mainly fishing, basking in the sun, trying to see game, plus general camp chores. You may - or may not - be bored.

Like wildfowling, the Zambesi Valley is an acquired taste. Personally, I love it. There's just that little flicker of danger to give flavour, but basically ones relationship with the big animals is a question of good manners. If you're hunting them they've every right to try and tread on you to my mind. In fact round 1 to them. As an old friend of mine who was starting up a series of foot safaris – cameras only – in Northern Rhodesia in days gone by once remarked. "My problem isn't teaching the <u>animals</u> good manners...

Had my first walk (with a gun) of the year last week, which produced 5 guinea fowl and 4 francolin – also sundry holes in the inoffensive atmosphere. Otherwise no great excitement here. Farm ticking over. Maize all reaped, fair crop. Tobacco 4/5 finished grading and selling and next years seedbeds sown and germinating. Early calving over – 64 with, I hope, another 108 coming in October. Hope to start planting next year's maize September 1ˢᵗ – under irrigation. And so life staggers on. Three of my mallard are sitting on eggs and a fourth pushed off by my b. dog and deserted. My writing gets worse and worse – au revoir and all good wishes. N

And finally

10ᵗʰ September

Dear Phil

Just a progress report to say all at present in order this end and will be expecting you at 0540 on 9ᵗʰ October at Salisbury airport. I'll almost certainly be there to meet you but if something untoward happens – eg. I turn the car over on the way in – take a bus from the airport to Meikles Hotel in Salisbury and get in touch with Corona by phone. Anyhow, all that is pure pessimism. C or I will be there.

Clothes; don't overburden yourself. Likely it'll be hot. 2 or 3 pairs of shorts, open necked shirts, NOT bright colours for choice! Canvas – or some floppy hat. Gym shoes, for walking. Couple of pairs of flannels – or jeans – one fairly respectable, t'other in case mosquitoes are bad at camp. One or two jerseys – it can be chilly when the sun goes down and that's about it. I'll lay on a blanket, stretcher, fleabag etc and you're not likely to need a dinner jacket or tails! If you want to bring anything for the commissariat bring a small Stilton cheese – or any cheese! Cheese has been non-existent over here for months and one jolly well misses a staple diet item. One small thing you might bring me. You'll have killed a partridge by now – lucky devil – I want a few dozen of the lower wing covert feathers for tying a certain fly called a "Walkers killer". It sometimes produces a nice rainbow (trout) for breakfast. More often it sticks up a tree on ones back cast!

Affairs here ticking over slowly at present – reasonably happily. Some desperate shortages – fuel and spare parts notably which could well have serious long term effects – particularly farming and land use, as simply not enough for maintenance – roads, contours, dams etc as well as basic cropping needs like ploughing.

Had an amusing stalk last week. A big bunch of baboons in the neighbourhood – really bad vermin and worse than geese to get near. A bunch of 80 – 100. Saw them half a mile away in the open – they'd also seen me of course. So, left my cattle boy – who was with me – to keep in their view. Did a long detour and came up from 180 degrees and got within 200 yards. A rather lucky shot took one a bit far back but stopped her. I have never taken a buck or anything at that range I may say. Only hope the rest of the gang take the hint and keep off Merryhill.   *As ever - Nigel*

Anyone who knows me would tell you that I am not interested in travel and still less in subjecting myself to close contact with masses of strangers at an airport or on the trains and underground to get even that far. It must therefore come as a surprise to those who know me well that I ever embarked on this journey at all. It was however, my first ever flight, I had not then had a taste of claustrophobic checking in queues and chaotic departure lounges and I really wanted to experience my friend's part of Africa. So, at 5.30pm on 8th October 1981 I set off from Gatwick on the Air Zimbabwe flight to Salisbury. It was still Salisbury then but the winds of change were already beginning to blow through that particular sector of the Dark Continent.

The aeroplane was a Boeing 737 and so pretty cramped for such a long haul flight. There was a scheduled stop at Frankfurt to take on some German passengers. As we flew in over the Belgian coast the rivers showed clearly as winding bands of silver as they reflected the light of the moon. It was easy to see why during the Second World War the RAF and Luftwaffe bomber squadrons chose such nights for their raids. Our mission this night however was benign and after forty-five minutes on German soil we took off again for the main part of the journey.

It was dark outside of course, but I took the Captain's word for it when he kept us informed of our position. "We are flying along Italy and if you look down to the right you will see the lights of Rome." In no time at all it seemed we had crossed the Med and were above North Africa. Good Lord, we're nearly there! I had yet to fully understand just how big Africa is. The aircraft was over Tripoli and crossing Chad at first light. The lightening from a distant thunderstorm flickered like flames across the morning clouds as we passed over Zambia and began a gradual descent. Before long we were low enough to see the red earth and sparse vegetation – even a few isolated clusters of round thatched huts. There was a lot more trees and scrub as we flew over the Zambesi River and its surrounding bushveldt. We had crossed the border into what had until recent months been Southern Rhodesia and were on the run in to Salisbury.

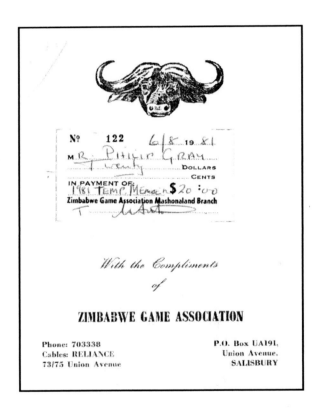

Zimbabwe Game Association - Hunters licence

3
Welcome to Rhodesia!

Salisbury airport at 7.00 am. We disembarked straight onto the tarmac where I immediately saw my first African birds – large black and white crows that were scavenging around at a safe distance. The other first impression was an Army officer in khaki shirt and shorts. Socks correctly just under the knee, peaked cap, swagger stick and bristling moustache. Oh yes, the remains of the disappearing colonial way of life.

While I waited for my luggage I kept an eye open for Nigel. He had said that if he hadn't made it to the Airport before I arrived I was to make my way to Meikles Hotel and wait there in the bar for him. That wasn't necessary though as I spotted his tall, long legged shape heading towards me with hand extended long before he reached me. "Welcome to Africa!" he beamed as we shook hands. "Glad you could make it."

We were not long driving out of the city that was soon to become Harare and then the whole of the sixty miles to Marrandellas was along single-track roads where we did not meet much traffic. If we did meet an occasional truck or car the drivers of both vehicles steered their nearside wheels over onto the dirt verges throwing up thick and choking clouds of red dust. In places we came across African people walking to work or school. It was strange to feel so warm at this time of the morning in October and as I wasn't driving I could look around and enjoy all the strange surroundings and birds, most of which Nigel had to identify for me. Not ten minutes from the airport we saw a yellow-billed eagle, then lots of kites hunting along the road much as our kestrel does. Red-rumped and red-breasted swallows we saw and even a few of our own swallows, newly arrived from the UK. It was interesting to meet them at the other end of their long migration. We turned into a dirt road that eventually led to "Merryhill" the Thornycroft farm and as we did so a red mongoose, rather like a red stoat, ran across in front of the car. We saw another just before we arrived at the house.

The low thatched roofs of the long white house and its outlying buildings peeped above the yellow grasses as we approached. There was some activity among the buildings so it was obvious we had been spotted. Corona had everyone lined up to meet me - Lovemore the cook, Josie the house-girl and Benson the garden-boy. To my slight embarrassment I was introduced as Baas (Boss) Philip, but apart from the welcoming gesture it had the purpose of letting them know who I was, why I was there and where I would be sleeping. After Corona and Richard, the youngest Thornycroft son, I shook hands with them all and we went into the house for breakfast. Insulated by the thatch, the house was pleasantly cool inside.

The outbuildings at Merryhill Farm, Rhodesia 1981

Richard stayed for breakfast over which we mulled over all the news both locally and from England.

28

The trade embargoes set up as a result of UDI had created many shortages and one of the minor ones, but keenly felt by the ex-pats was the lack of cheese. Three items I had been asked to bring with me were a new Hardy Trout rod, which Nigel had ordered and had delivered to my home, a consignment of dyes which Corona had ordered for her cottage industry of making greetings cards and calendars from local grasses and bird feathers and as large as stilton cheese as I could manage within the weight limits of my luggage! A friend of mine who had met Nigel on one of his visits had asked me to take an oil painting of a wild rabbit. To protect this in transit I had built a simple box around it with strips of wood and hardboard. The hardboard had been nailed to the wood with several brass panel pins. The rod I had protected by inserting it into a length of plastic drainpipe plugged at each end with a wooden bung. That the Thornycroft's were almost as excited by the brass pins and plastic pipe as the contents brought home to me just how difficult things must have been. As for the Stilton, well that was unwrapped with joy and treated with reverence for as long as it lasted. Nigel's first act was to scoop out the top and pour in a good measure of port. I think it gave me almost as much pleasure watching my friends enjoy that cheese as the pleasure they got eating it.

The Thornycrofts had decided to farm here in the Wedza District at the end of the war and took over the land, which had upon it a few tobacco barns and a borehole for the water supply. From there they started from scratch. Nigel had come out first and made a start on things and a heavily pregnant Corona with another babe in arms had made a stressful journey to join her husband wearing a fur coat, because it was winter when she departed and carrying along with everything else, a brace of pheasants which Nigel had insisted be brought out to some elderly relatives of his. Not surprisingly, by the time they reached their destination the birds were so "high" they were promptly binned.

The house and eventual other buildings were built of upright gum tree poles, which were then plastered with dagga, in other words wattle and daub. The mud walls were at least a foot thick, perhaps more. More poles formed the shape of the roof. These poles were crossed with bamboo and wire and then thickly thatched with bundles of long grass. The whole place was whitewashed inside and out. Over the years various improvements were added and an ancient boiler now provided hot water for the kitchen and bathroom. In the lounge area was a built in hearth and the room was decorated with scenes of the North Norfolk Coast. There was also a large Peter Scott print of Shoveller and a pair of Garganey rising from a Norfolk reed bed. In the office was a massive safe, which must have weighed half a ton and to my delight, the very gun cupboard that Nigel had described in *"Fowler's Moon"*! Some of the contents were different now of course. No great 8 bore stood in the baize-lined racks, but a 12 bore by Purdey was there and that was the gun that did most of Nigel's shooting in the 1920's and 30's. There was a nice little .410 that Corona had owned as a young girl, a 7mm rifle for antelope and the like and to cope with bigger game like buffalo and elephant, a heavy express rifle.

After breakfast I was shown to the guest sleeping quarters, which was a delightful little round hut built, as was the house except that the roof poles here were fixed in a wigwam fashion. Half a tree for a shelf, two windows, each a foot square let in the light. A bed, an armchair, a chest of drawers and a couple of trunks made up the furniture of this happy little place. Among the other buildings was a large barn like place, which turned out to be Corona's workroom. Here, a dozen African girls giggled as they worked on the card production. All the buildings and the gardens were surrounded by an eight-foot high chain linked compound fence, the defences against possible terrorist attacks during their recent war. No thoughts of fighting now however, while I changed, Nigel was trying out his new rod on the lawn.

After an interval of half an hour Nigel invited me to drive around some of the farm with him. I learned that the first land they bought was the part they called "checwere" and when after several years' things were going well, they had dug out the foundations for their proposed mansion. I was taken to the site of which, all that remained was an overgrown hole in the ground. "That." Said Nigel. "Was to be my wine cellar, but then our neighbour wanted to sell up so we took a deep breath and bought him out. We doubled the size of our farm to 6000 acres, but it put on hold any dreams of a mansion." The neighbour's farm had been called "Sheffield" a name they still used.

Nigel explained that 200 – 300 acres were down to maize, 5000 acres was rough grazing and the remaining 700-800 acres grew tobacco. We stopped at the tobacco barns, which were the first building erected on taking on the farm. The timbers for these were mature gum trees sawn in sawpits. The bricks were made of puddled soil from anthills, moulded and dried in the sun and then burned.

The barns play a crucial part in the tobacco production. In these building the leaves are cured, steam pressed, graded and baled. I was shown a small wire frame with twenty-seven sprung-loaded gaps along its length. Three tobacco leaves are held in each gap and the frames are hung up in the curing shed.

As we drove through the grazing areas we passed plantations of hundreds of gum trees. Nigel first planted them as wind breaks but the gum is a far more useful tree than just that. It grows quickly and it grows tall and straight so it can be cut at various stages of its growth depending whether you require three inch diameter poles fence rails, house timbers or telegraph poles. Not only that, apparently the tree can be felled once and then will grow again from the same stump. After the second felling the stumps are used for firewood at the tobacco curing sheds. As the wood dries out so it hardens. The timbers of the old barns were like oak but that did not prevent the boring bees from drilling a neat ½ inch diameter hole into them.

Leaving the barns we moved on through the maize, which was in its earliest stages of growth. It is from time to time damaged in turn by Kudu, monkeys, baboons or wild pig. In letters to me Nigel has described sessions of lying in wait for these marauders and what better than to print one here for the benefit of the reader. This one is dated 6th – 13th January 1982.

Dear Phil

I've been thinking of you over the last few nights and rather chuckling to myself over possible contrasts in the scenes the moon was showing us.

We're having a bit of a war on our hands here at the moment. Crops are well up – tobacco topped and suckered and the earlier stuff just starting to show signs of ripening. We shall, in fact be taking our first reapings from Monday on; and the maize ten feet high and cobs plumping out. Well, a troop of a hundred or so baboons have been treating us to sporadic raids. They have a dear habit of walking in to a tobacco land, breaking a plant off a foot or so from the ground, peeling back the skin of the broken stalk, taking a nibble at the soft centre and discarding the rest to move on to the next plant and repeat. A hundred baboons can make a v. big mess in a v. short time. I reckon we've lost 7 – 8 acres already. They may come in once a week at any hour of the day, almost like trained troops with vedettes and scouts out, wreak chaos in half an hour or so and beat it for the horizon. I did get one some weeks ago, which dampened their ardour for a few days, but they've been back several times since and only once have we seen them – at a quarter mile distance. We accelerated their departure with a couple of magazines of FN bullets but more in rage than hope. They've now discovered the maize – well. And, the kudu are starting on the tobacco. At least they're beautiful animals and I'd hate to have to get rough with them. Odd, isn't it? Yet I can spend days cheerfully and happily trying to get one in the (*Zambesi*) valley.

And now pigs – probably the biggest scourge and hardest to cope with of the three as they're virtually nocturnal and often take up residence in the maize land itself. And if you can picture 250 acres of ten-foot high maize stalks growing in rows at six-inch intervals and rows three feet apart, needles in haystacks become easy meat. The pigs just smash stuff down

32

taking a bite of a cob here and another there and the resulting mess has to be seen to be believed.

Which brings me back to my opening paragraph. Lying up for pig under the moon can be a damned exciting game. This current chapter started about five days ago when I saw fresh tracks leading up from the river and followed in to see what sort of a mess they were making. I saw all right – but what I didn't expect to see was a glimpse of the creators of the mess through about six rows of maize stalks, just standing. I could just see a strip of his face through the jungle and I doubt if he was five yards off. But alas, he heard the click of the rifle cocking and wheeled of like a flash – even so I'm not sure how I missed him, but couldn't find any blood.

Still, my blood was up by now, as there must have been a dozen or more there from the noise of the stampede – and the damage they were doing. So I snuck down just before dusk, found a narrow channel across the rows where an irrigation pipe had lain and a cross row I could see down and lay down flat. It's a mysterious game. You're virtually in a tunnel, with the maize stalks meeting ten feet above your head and a narrow strip of sky where the pig had knocked stuff down. Ears at fullest stretch and mouth half open to listen more keenly. A touch of breeze and the leaves rustle together and you tense – is it a pig brushing against them? A big beetle blunders by and hits a leave quite close – it could well be a pig snapping a stalk fifty yards away and you tense again. A bunch small birds frrip in the maize tops – what direction was that? Thunder in the distance – and then that first night the pat pat pat of big drops startlingly loud – followed by the deluge and a dripping figure squelching to its feet and back to the car. It's astonishing how easy it is to follow a narrow track through maize by day and how easy it is to miss that same narrow track in the darkness.

The next night everything seemed perfect still, and without a breath to rustle the maize leaves and you could have heard a piglet breath a hundred yards away or a snapped stalk at half a mile. Also a three-quarter moon peeping out of the clouds to sharpen visibility on the ground. But – never a piglet breathed nor a maize stalk snapped though I hung on 'til nearly 9 o'clock. Only mosquitoes – that utterly maddening pinggg and you daren't slap – just in case.

Then last night. It had rained half the day and the evening was that damp and breathless harbinger of more thunder to come. Tiny puffs of breeze from all round the compass. Made a cautious approach and snuck in about 6.00 pm. Masses of swallows flying over high and then the odd flock of quelias as the light was going. Then, within half an hour – patter pat- sniff – rustle – silence – more pattering – a tiny grunt – definitely coming closer – they couldn't be ten yards away and – any second now…

A louder snoof – scurried stampede – and silence. Had they departed? A rustle and a single step, almost on top of me – a louder, more confident snoof – a scurry and silence – utter and complete. And that was that – leaving me almost wobbly weak and mildly sweating.

I stayed another hour, not really hoping, lying on my back and watching the maize leaf tracery above. A guinea fowl, disturbed at roost, scolded from beyond the river. Mosquitoes pinged. How the devil do they find you, and in your absence, what to they eat? Then crack – literally from behind my head – maize stalk pushed over and crunch crunch crunch. No doubt who that was. Infinitely slowly I did a hundred and eighty degree turn. Snuffle, rustle, patter of feet – closer – another crash and crunch crunch crunch. Couldn't have been five yards away but the stalks were black and thick together. Then again – that long drawn out snoof – and silence. Just on the chance I lay with the gun at my shoulder pointing down the two foot wide gap I'd come in by – and for a second it was blotted and I fired and he'd made his last mistake and was kicking on the ground with a dozen SSG pellets in his face and neck. Feeling rather weak I tried to drag him, but with half a mile to go in the dark, gave up.

He was there this morning and on the scale went 168 lbs. Probably no record breaker but a pretty solid bunch of bone and muscle. Honour is satisfied; I shall not go out tonight!
----------N.

Maize is the staple diet of the African as well as being used for cattle food so it is an important crop to the country and its neighbours. It looked good at the time I was there, the field with its carpet of big green leaves stretching away for acres and with Wedza Mountain solidly guarding the horizon.

We came into the coarse yellow grass of the rough grazing. Acres and acres slightly rolling and dotted with clumps of bushes and kopjes. Several individuals of a graceful little antelope called steenbok made an appearance. At a guess I would say they are about the same size as "our" munjac but of more slender build. Nigel said. "We'll just have a look at a dam up here." Ah. I would at last know at first hand what he meant by the term. It was simple really; in places where rainwater ran off a slope in one part a low bank was build across the base to dam the run–off point. This conserved valuable water for some time after the rains had ceased. There was a little shallow water in the one we inspected and using it were wattled plover, ringed plover, greenshank, striped swallow, red-breasted swallow and even a small cormorant. The loose feathers drifting on and around the waters edge disclosed the recent presence of duck. One of the side benefits of these dams is that they provide some occasional duck shooting. Nigel said that there are no real statutory shooting seasons for duck; the landowners use their own judgement. If the birds have had a bad breeding season no one shoots, whereas in good years they decide what a reasonable harvest will be and stick to it, ceasing shooting well before the nesting time.

The next dam we visited was created by putting in a spillover dam across a small river. The river could run through it but the waters above the dam spread to fill a low valley creating a fair sized lake. On a slope rising from this lake, which was known as Scott's dam the Thornycrofts, were building a house. Half a dozen African men were working on it while women were busy gathering and drying grass for thatch. I commented at the time that it would be a lovely place to live when completed. Over a decade later my son Robert was to visit and stayed with Corona in that very house. On our way back to the house we met one of Nigel's workers an old cattle minder. The two conversed for a few moments in Shona – the local tongue and then we left the old fellow to his business while we headed for lunch.

After the meal, a sleep to recover from the effects of the long flight and the change in altitude – this part of central Africa is on a plateau 5000 feet above sea level and to a fenman normally living near or even below sea level, the difference is considerable! I was roused for tea taken under an oak in the garden while we watched thirty mallard cavorting in a small pond. These duck have the run of the place and one had a nest right under the window of Nigel's office. Near the gates of the compound fence close by a grove of bamboo, was a thatched carport. In the bamboo hung many nests of the masked weaverbird, a beautiful little yellow bird with a black face. The male builds the nest of woven grasses some six inches deep and four in diameter. The entrance is towards the bottom and the whole thing is fixed to its branch or reed by a small binding of grass. If the female doesn't like the nest she snips through the binding so that it falls to the ground and the poor old cock bird has to start all over again. Corona brought one of the discarded nests for me to inspect. It looked fine to me but that's a female for you!

Later we all drove around so that I could see the Country Club resplendent with is Dutch gables and newly thatched roof and avenue of vivid blue jacaranda trees. Then, avoiding an ant bears hole in the dirt road, we viewed a new Church that was being built nearby. Our route eventually took us down to the site of the new house where we parked. While Corona collected grasses for her cards Nigel and I took a canoe out onto the dam. It was a fascinating place. We paddled past twelve-foot high reeds hung with quite literally hundreds of weaverbirds nests. The brilliant masked weavers again and another species too. We stalked and got within fifteen yards of a squacco heron before it took wing. I managed to snap a photograph of this interesting buff, creamy coloured bird, but sadly not having the benefit of a zoom lens it did not show up very well on the resulting print. Pied kingfisher hovered and dived sending up splashes of water in all directions. Swallows skimmed the surface and Black Duck and White faced duck flew in overhead. At the end of the dam from a high kopje, flew a pair of hammerkopf. Strange looking birds looking like a weird cross between a harrier, a mottled gull and a heron. The feathers sticking out from the back of its head really do make it look like the head of a hammer. We saw a lily-hopper which is more or less a large moorhen, red and blue waxbills, Jacobin cuckoo, kuckow and a go 'way bird. As we paddled back to the shore the first twenty white little egrets glided in to the reeds on the far side of the lake. On beaching the boat we found that Richard, with two bottles of wine, had joined Corona. As we sat there with our relaxing drink, a further forty egrets joined the others to roost along with over sixty cormorants, a great white heron and a purple heron. There was talk of a leopard that had killed eleven calves over a short period of time on a neighbouring farm. "One can put up with a few calves being taken". Commented Nigel. "But she is pushing her luck." We stayed on under the trees with the mosquitoes and a background chorus of frogs and night birds until it was well dark, the moon had risen and the two bottles were empty. While we sat quietly absorbing all the small noises that make up the silence of the night there came a sound that puzzled me. It was something like a cross between the distant booming of a bittern and the rumbling of a disgruntled bull. "Oh, that's Cassius, our neighbours lion." Richard casually explained.

Later that night I was in my hut writing up my diary of the events of the day before preparing for bed when a bird began to call. I opened the door onto a silver grey scene as the bright moon flooded the compound with its dim light with the shadows throwing the house and other buildings into bold relief. It was very quiet and still except for my bird which every few moments made its beautiful whistling call. "Whip–Whip-

Whip-poor-Will" is the best attempt I can make to describe the sound it made. It seemed to wait for a reply before calling again but if it got one my ears were not good enough to pick it up. I stood in my doorway for some time listening to the bird but never did see it. In the end all was quiet once more and I retired to my bed.

Being an early riser, the early to bed, early to rise lifestyle of my friends suited me very well. The house girl brought my first cup of tea of the day punctually at 5.20 every morning. I was out at 7.00 on this morning and had walked a couple of miles or so along the dirt roads towards the tobacco barns and had almost reached the African workers compound when Nigel turned up in the battered and ancient Renault 5 which served as the farm car. "I'm off back for breakfast – want a lift?" Over coffee after breakfast Nigel showed me his game book dating back to the 1920's and featuring of course, some wildfowling venues well known to me. There were articles by Corona and himself that had been published in *The Field.* "Lord, but its good to have you here." He smiled. "It is bringing back so many good memories." I told him of the avian visitor of the previous night and when I described the call he identified the bird as an African Nightjar. I wondered, considering the sound of its call, whether this bird was related to what the Americans call a whip-poor-will?

Corona then showed me photographs of an archaeological dig she had carried out on an African burial found on the farm. A woman crouched on her side, two pots buried with her and smashed with a rock. The body had been buried under a cairn of stones in an attempt to protect it from scavengers. Corona was involved in the recording of rock paintings for the Rhodesian Museum Society. 2000 years ago Bushmen had peopled the area. These primitive people lived on the kopjes and painted pictures of themselves and the animals they saw and hunted onto the rock, just as did the Stone Age cave dwellers.

We drove some three miles to such a kopje on the farm. Walking through a standing of gum trees we came to the pile of massive rocks that stand one on top of another seemingly precarious but standing for centuries. They were left standing as the soil was eroded around them thousands of years ago. The granite has split in many cases and it is amazing how they remain standing. We scrambled up this kopje to a place where the base of the rock sloped inwards. Under this shelter were the paintings on the smooth rock face the "paint" was red ochre and after all that time the pictures are still very clear. Reedbuck, Kudu, Elephant, and other antelopes were all recognised by Corona. I knew the Elephant! The human figures, hunting scenes, men with bows and arrows. It was all so clear.

Moving higher up we came to a flat level space. I was shown the still visible evidence of a hut. There was still broken pottery and even a crude corn grinding stone all lying about on the surface 2000 years on! Even with a cursory glance I could see that it would be a good place to have a dwelling. At least twenty feet off the ground, secure from immediate threat from prowling predators. A back wall of solid rock and a forward panoramic view of perhaps 130 degrees made it a well chosen site for the home of a bushman and his family.

Corona leads the way up a Kopje

As we scrambled down Corona stopped near a gap between two rocks to point out some human bones. They were the remains of a Shona burial that had been unearthed by a porcupine. There were plenty of signs of the dassie, or rock rabbit. They look like an overgrown guinea pig. One or two peered at us from behind the rocks. Nearby was the nest of a pair of Hammerkopf, which resembled an incredibly huge pile of old sticks and branches.

Our way back took us by Richard's house so we dropped in for a cold drink. The interior of the house was wonderfully cool. On the floor was a wildebeeste skin rug and draped over the back of the sofa was a leopard skin. Whether or not that gave Corona an idea to make things exciting for me I do not know, but when she was telling Richard what we had been doing she said. " While we were up the Kopje we went very quietly past the leopards hole." Perhaps I am being unkind and cynical for there <u>were</u> leopards taking calves in the area and holes in Kopjes are a favourite lair for the animal so, who knows? She may not have been pulling my leg after all.

Leaving Richard sorting out some of last year's tobacco we returned to the farmhouse for a lunch of avocados and lemons from the garden. Richard was organising the ridging in preparation for planting this season's tobacco and during the afternoon Nigel and I, on our way to another part of the farm, drove past the field. We lurched to a halt near a stand of gum trees and negotiating one of the barbed wire gates, known by some I believe, as Australian gates, made our way down to a kopje, which overlooked a low vlei. In the valley, which was three-quarters of a mile across were some of Nigel's Herefords with calves. My host had brought a rifle with him, as there had been a calf-stealing jackal around. For an hour we sat with our backs against a boulder watching the cattle browse down to a dam. The jackal did not put in an appearance, neither for that matter did the baboons which also "come visiting" from across the valley. What we did see at this beautiful spot was a glorious glossy starling and the steen buck, duiker and a pair of reedbuck.

It transpired that the kopje near which we sat was once home to a she leopard, which had raised her cubs there for a few years. They took a calf or two but kept down the monkeys and baboons. Nigel opined that the odd calf had been deemed a fair rent in the circumstances and the leopard had been left to her own devices.

That evening we drove over to the neighbouring farm and home of the Traver's, good friends of the Thornycrofts. The house was a mansion of the type that Nigel had aspired to, but then this family were in their second or third generation. In the garden there were two cheetahs, a wart hog, bush pigs, a leopard, an elephant and Cassius, the lion I had heard the previous evening. I should say that the Traver's set aside part of their farm as a game park and that these "house pets" were enclosed inside fenced runs within the garden.

I was shown around by Richard and Johnny Travers. Richard said. "What do think of this?" as he drew back a curtain to reveal a large black eagle perching on the window ledge. We were called to supper and as it was the occasion of Norman Travers 60th Birthday it was a "black tie" affair and there were several other guests. The ladies were escorted in until there were sixteen of us seated at the table of a room hung with magnificent skins of Zebra, Sable, Kudu and the like. A massive elephant tusk ornamented one end of the room and buffalo heads adorned the porch. Candles by the score flickered, reflecting light from the polished table and the silver. Four African servants stood to attention on each side of the room ready top up glasses or bring in the next course. David Hamilton, a long time friend, gave an amusing tribute to Norman and how he had managed to live to the age of sixty.

I sat next Natalie Seago who I had escorted in to the meal. This lady was a widow whose husband had been killed during the recent fighting. Bravely she carried on running her ranch even though she lost 1000 head of cattle to marauding terrorists. They wanted meat, but incredibly they left her alone. At the time I spoke to her she still had 2000 head of cattle on 13,000 acres. The cattle ranches, because of the poor quality of the grazing need to consist of a huge acreage of land. As a result the homesteads are very isolated indeed. How many people do you know who would live on their own in a location like that with bands of pretty desperate customers roaming about?

The ladies left us to the brandy and cigars during which time I learned more about these tough people. The oldest guest was Andrew Young and he was keen to talk to a fellow fenman. He was born in the Lincolnshire port of Boston and came out to Rhodesia in 1925. "The last time I was in Boston my boy." He said. "The cabs were still horse drawn!"

We re-joined the ladies for charades followed by some entertaining and somewhat sadistic games dreamed up by Richard. For example, a game of blow football where the pitch was a tray of water. Of course it ended with the referee – Richard, who else? slapping the water and soaking the players. At the end of the evening came the "one for the road" game where everyone joined one of two teams to collect items on a list drawn up by the host. The winners being the first team to gather all the listed items. The list, from what I can remember, included a left hand silk stocking, a hair from the elephants tail, a bristle from a bush pig, a pair of silk panties, a hair from Cassius, a tick from the chui (leopard) etc etc. Everyone dashed out into darkness of the garden. Barbie Travers went to

Cassius's enclosure and this great fully grown thickly maned African lion who has known Barbie since she was a child walking him around the farm, ambled over and rubbed along the chain link fence purring like an old tomcat. This purr however, sounded more like a pneumatic drill. I stroked his back and stole some of his hair as he passed, but I was the other side of the wire. The drink wasn't <u>that</u> strong! He really was a lovely beast. I think all of the items were collected, even the tick, but naturally nobody knew, nor cared who had won. Home by 1.30 am and the house girl still brought the tea tray at 5.30 am.

4

Game lands & Shark hooks

Sunday morning. After the morning tea I joined Nigel who was going to supervise the loading of twenty-five head of cattle that were due for slaughter. At the loading ramp the boys had the beasts penned ready to load but – no lorry to be seen. A phone call to the transport company revealed that the driver was drunk and hadn't turned up for work. With a replacement promised in forty-five minutes we could do nothing but head back for breakfast. When the cattle were eventually loaded and on their way we changed and went into Salisbury to watch a test match between Zimbabwe and the West Indies. The sun glared fiercely, whitely, hotly off the pavements while some of the streets were a sea of colour with avenues of vivid blue jacaranda trees in full bloom. At the match it rained for a while, but it wouldn't be cricket without a spot of the wet stuff. At least it brought a refreshing coolness and it being only a shower, we were able to enjoy most of the days play.

By 6.30 am the next morning I was out for a walk along the farm roads. I was still not above 100 yards from the house when I saw a striped swallow and then a black necked snake eagle. The eagle soared around then shut its wings swooping steeply down to earth, not so very far from me. Moments later, when it rose, I could see something I could not identify, hanging limply from its bill. The bird had obviously spotted and targeted its unfortunate quarry and soared round to come into the wind.
Coming across a grove of gum trees I left the road and wandered over some scrubby grazing land. As I came out of the trees a golden oriole flew in the opposite direction. The land sloped gently down and I found myself looking across the vlei to a cluster of grass thatched, round native huts. There was a steady flow of women walking down the slope on their side of

the valley. They walked very erect as they carried pitchers on their heads. When I spotted some making the return journey up the slope I twigged what was happening. Through my binoculars I saw the flash and glitter where a stream ran through the vlei. They were fetching their first batch of water of the day.

The snake eagle flew over to pitch on an old maize stubble. Instantly it was mobbed by a pair of crested plover who, no doubt, had young nearby. I was taking in the scene before me when the blast of a car horn rudely interrupted my thoughts. Guessing I was wanted, I headed back. Before I got to the road Nigel drove past in a cloud of dust without spotting my approach. By the time I reached the house he had had breakfast and was in a hurry to get to Marrandellas.

I soon swallowed my breakfast and we were on our way. Our first port of call was the small local hospital where we dropped off Tikki (*Sixpence*), one of the farm boys. Tikki had trapped his foot in the hydraulic lifting gear of a tractor two days previously and the swelling had not gone down.

From the hospital to the abattoir seems a strange move but that's where we pitched up in time to see the beasts we loaded yesterday go through the system from walking in one end and coming out at the other as half carcasses. They were graded on a weight for length of vertebrae formula, which results in a fat layer figure. "Our" beast's grade out 100% grade 1 on the fat layer but A, B or C grading overall. The number of teeth is recorded and a full-mouthed bullock had points deducted if it did not meet other criteria. In case of arguments the head of each animal travelled round on a separate track so any disputes could be easily settled. Obviously there had been some in the past!

Next stop the Town Centre and a gun shop to pick up some 7mm ammunition. It was very much more expensive than in Britain. The proprietor was a dour Scot who mournfully commiserated with Nigel over the price but didn't offer any discount. A visit to the bank and the post office completed our list before we drove home.

With lunch and a decent interval behind us we took Richard down to his house to collect his motorbike. There was a board some twelve inches square bolted to rest on the pillion. My curiosity as to its purpose wasn't stretched for long for, at the sound of the bike starting up a Jack Russell terrier appeared from nowhere and leapt onto the board. This was "Jaws." Apparently the little dog loved to ride and did so at every opportunity. We followed Richard along the dirt roads. He was travelling at least 30mph and Jaws swayed about like a sailor in a rough sea with his feet nailed to the deck. At the site of the new house Nigel and Corona had a brief dispute over the location of a doorway into a room. When agreement was reached they simply instructed the African workers to knock a doorway through in the desired position and brick up the original one. No planning permission or building regulations here. You could almost make it up as you went along!

Nigel at the rivers edge ready to fill the bait boxes with damp soil

Leaving Richard there the three of us drove to a river that ran through the farm. We had come with large wooden boxes, which we filled with damp earth from the river's edge. This was to be storage for worms, bait for fishing at the camp near the Zambesi.

On a nearby kopje Corona pointed out some Bushman paintings. In a tree not far away I spotted a beautiful black-shouldered kite. The drive back had its moments too. We had seen black cuckoo, jacobin cuckoo, duiker and steenbok and then, when I got out of the car to open a gate, from the waist high yellow grass and not more than ten feet from me, clattered an enormous dark and speckled bird like a lightweight emu. As it flew I pointed and spluttered not able to get the words out. "Black Korhaan," grinned Nigel, replying to my un-uttered question. It was a magnificent bird of the bustard family. As if that wasn't enough, we came across five kudu – four cows with a young bull, as big as donkeys, but more beautiful by far. They stood for a few seconds before silently vanishing like ghosts. Without seeming to move they just merged and filtered into the background.

Early the next morning found us looking at some of the cattle. Herefords, gradually being crossed with Afrikander bulls, were being turned out into fresh paddocks. A "paddock" here could be over 400 acres. We noticed that one cow was limping badly and on investigation found that its hind leg had been caught in a snare. The marks made by the wire noose were clearly visible. Poor old Nyson the head cattle boy got a rocket for putting her back out after he had removed the wire. Nigel's temper was not improved when he found evidence of sapling stripping in one of his plantations. The long strips of bark are peeled off by African women and used for tying bundles of firewood. They called it, and any other tying material, as far as I could tell; "Tambor" The problem of course, is that it kills the trees. Nyson, no doubt protecting his friends, said that the women had come from a neighbouring village.

The last straw for Nigel was when we drove homewards we had to stop for a large hole that had been dug in the middle of the road to excavate a wild bees nest. "I do wish the bastards would fill it in when they get what they want!" he swore.

Breakfast revived my friend's normally good humour and while Corona drove in to Salisbury to purchase worms, our bait for the Zambesi fish, Nigel took me over to *Imire* the Travers' farm. As we approached along the dusty farm road I spotted a secretary bird stalking about in the grass. We were actually on Johnny Traver's part of the estate, 2000 acres set aside as a game park. As the car crunched to a halt outside their bungalow Johnny's wife Judy appeared to greet us and offered to show us around. A tame Impala and a steenbok peered gentle eyed, at us from the garden.

The place is large enough for all the animals to be completely wild and free. Impala, eland, wildebeest and zebra all roamed and grazed. A group of tsessebe – the fastest of all the antelopes – stood alert near the still water of a dam along with some reedbuck and waterbuck We saw the magnificent, and dangerous sable antelope lurking in a clearing amid some scrub land. Great horns swept back, curving like scimitars. Not far from them three giraffe stalked about, graceful despite their long legs and necks.

Driving down into a vlei we found ourselves amid a mixed herd of zebra and buffalo. One old bull with a mighty boss between his horns came within 20 feet of the car; head back, peering over his nostrils as he sniffed the air to see what we were. Nigel, I was relieved to see, had kept the engine running.

49

The old car had been playing up and we had had to push start it three or four times. I didn't fancy repeating the operation just now. At a small dam a crocodile dozed, looking mean and ugly even in its somnolent state. Birds galore, at every turn – Roller, "Our" Cuckoo, Waxbill and hornbill.

We came out onto a high kopje overlooking a splendid scene. Across the vlei to high ground and mountains, including Wedza mountain in the distance. Closer to hand was a rock formation known as the "lion's head." I seemed to have heard of "lions heads" all over Africa, starting with those in Rider–Haggard's writings, but this rock certainly looked like one. It was very hot by this time so we drove Judy home and after thanking her for her hospitality, took our leave.

On our drive back to Merryhill Nigel showed me a high fence that came up to the main road on either side. It turned out that when the Travers' want to move a sable or two over into the other part of the park they completely fence off the main road in two places and erect notices saying "Stop – game crossing" As Nigel said. Where else in the world could you do that? He explained that when there is a surplus of sable they move a few over into the hunting area of the park. Rich Americans come over and would pay $500 to shoot a sable antelope. Norman Travers does it well for them. Though he knows pretty well where the beasts are he takes the clients hunting the spoor for about three days until, on the last day they "come up with" the sable and get their shot. The Rhodesians do take liberties with their roads. They fenced off some 500 yards of the road in a similar fashion down in the South of the country when Nigel's son Mike flew a light aircraft into a farm, landing on the road with 6 inches to spare either side.

After lunch that day I relaxed with my friends Game Books, which dated back to the 1920's and found some interesting entries. Corona's book was illustrated with beautiful little pen and ink sketches, sometimes coloured in to highlight some red-letter day or event. Her father was Philip Hammond Gurney who ran the Maltings at Narborough near Kings Lynn, Norfolk. Corona has shot since she was 14 years old and fished before that. She has led a very adventurous life, which included shooting an elk during a stay in Finland from June to November 1935. She would have been about 24 at the time.

When Peter Scott was living at the East Lighthouse at Sutton Bridge, Lincolnshire before the second World War, both Nigel and Corona went punt-gunning out in the Wash with the famous artist. Nigel had been at Cambridge with Scott and they had often shot together. One entry in Corona's Game Book is of a day when she was gunner and Scott the puntsman. They got a shot at a company of wigeon and the bag is recorded as 10 wigeon, 1 front tooth. She had got just too near the breech of the big gun when it recoiled.

After a siesta I awoke to the sounds of thunder and the pattering of rain and on entering the house I found Nigel's mood almost as grey as the sky. He had been packing some kit ready for our trip to the Zambesi Valley and found that much of his fishing hooks and line had been stolen. He brightened up over supper however and we enjoyed a sundowner while Corona showed some slides she had taken on past camps in bush of the Valley.

The next day was Wednesday 14th October 1981 and we were out and about pretty early on. 5.40 am found us at the bottom of a slope to join Richard watching a massive plough working its way down hill following the contours of the field. This ridging, almost terracing, is done to form a ditch to carry the water quickly off the land when the expected rains eventually arrive. Six inches of rain in twenty-four hours is not uncommon and if the ridges were not in place most of the soil would be washed off the fields.

A quick drive to the barns so that Nigel could telephone a rep. to ascertain the chances of ordering some fertilizer and then back to re-join Richard who was, with a theodolite, taking levels for further contour ridging. I wandered down a vlei from the roadside. Jaws, no doubt thinking I was after something, soon joined me and hopefully inspected every ant bear's hole. He was disappointed though for after 15 minutes Nigel called me back so that we could drive to the main road to collect a dozen cans of insecticide that had been dropped off.

We had deposited the cans in a shed near the house and were in the middle of breakfast when Richard came roaring up on his motorbike. While we finished the remains of the meal we went over the preparations for the Zambesi camp. One item we needed on the list was a fair amount of petrol. So breakfast over, we all went down to the barns again to the fuel store. I was intrigued to see that the only window was an iron wheel whose spokes formed effective bars. This and no less than five locks was the necessary security to protect the petrol, which was almost impossible to get hold of. Needless to say, if it were left unguarded it would soon be stolen.

Two cattle boys rode with us to *Sheffield* where we were going to count some cattle through the dip. 423 bellowing, dusty, heaving beasts went through and were mustered dripping, in a corral at the far end. From there after inspection, they where driven out to the respective paddocks by two of the cattle boys. The other two came back with us. One of the latter, and old grey bearded man with hair like white cotton wool, we dropped off near some ruined farm buildings. Nyson, the head cattle boy stayed on board.

Drawing to a halt near some gum trees Nigel showed me an experimental plot of coarse hardy plants, which it was hoped would spread throughout the local grass as a supplement, much as clover does in Britain. The experiment had been going on for two years at that time and had shown early signs of re-seeding and spreading. "We have got to do something to reduce the hand feeding costs." Commented my host. Not long after we had left the plot we got a puncture in the nearside front wheel. No tools were left on the vehicle because of theft and it was three or four miles back to the barns. We turned out the dogs while Nyson and I put all our weight on the offside rear wheel. We made the barns all right, but Richard saw what we were doing and was furious in case the wheel rim had been damaged. Luckily, though slightly marked it continued to serve its purpose after the puncture had been repaired. For the time being we merely changed to the spare and called at Richard's house to pick up a couple of rods and an additional reel. A long, cool, iced drink in the kitchen there was just the ticket after our dusty drive.

After our siesta there was the exciting business of sorting out rods, tackle, guns and ammunition for our departure the next day. The heaps of kit and luggage grew and I noticed that Nigel had not forgotten his box containing 500 Berkley cigarettes. He decided that a couple of shark hooks that hung in the one of the barns could be made into serviceable gaffs. On arrival at the barns – no hooks. "I've got a bloody good idea where we'll find them." He said as he strode purposefully off towards the African compound. I caught up with him because I was interested to see the huts. There are a hundred families on the farm and they live in a small hamlet of huts that had been provided by the Thornycrofts. Built with hand made bricks and with roofs of corrugated iron, each had windows, fireplace and chimney. We entered one or two and the occupants were asked about the missing hooks. Blank looks, appeasing grins and murmured "Nooo baas. No sin him." Was all their employer could get out of them, until eventually a young man came over having "found" them. As we left the compound Nigel commented "We built those huts for them and the first thing they do is block up the fireplace, make a hole in the roof and make their fire in the middle of the floor, as they would in their native huts. They also block up the windows." "Why do they do that?" "They're frightened that evil spirits will get into the house. It was a bit annoying at first, but when we thought about it and understanding how their minds work, we let them do as they liked. It is so irritating when you're press criticise us as wicked colonials exploiting the poor native. The perception is that the African here is on the same level as Jamaicans in the UK. They're not. The average West Indian is at least as intelligent as the average Brit, in many cases more so, but the people here are a good two hundred years behind the West. To expect these chaps to think as we do is like bringing a farm worker from 17th century England into the modern day. They wouldn't be able to cope with all the change. Our system here is very like the old feudal system in medieval times. We rely on our workers and they rely on us. They and their children are fed and clothed and get a wage. We could not afford to pay a hundred families a wage that our government thinks they ought to have. If it was insisted upon we would have to lay them off and the result of that would be the end of our farm, no food crops for the country and the laid off families would starve. There's no Social Security handouts here you know!" In the workshop at the barns we just had time to file off the barbs from the huge hooks before heading for supper.

Over supper and afterwards with a sundowner I heard stories of how the farmers had organised themselves into defensive units during their war. In 1977 everyone up to the age of 38 put in eighteen weeks annually in the army, ages 38 to 50 in police reserve and the ancients, as Nigel put it, filled in the gaps in business and production. Their own local area had been under the command of Norman Travers. One night Nigel was returning home from one of their strategy meetings at the Country Club when he was ambushed. He was driving the battered old Renault 5 with its one working sidelight and so was driving pretty slowly. On hearing banging and thumping noises behind him he though the back axle was succumbing to the rough dirt road. It was only when he turned to look over his shoulder and saw tracer bullets flickering across the road that he realised what was happening! He put his foot down and a couple of hundred yards on drove the car off the road, switched off the lights and fumbled desperately at the zip of the case containing his 7mm rifle. Then, remembering that he had only four rounds, thought better of it and drove to Richard's house. Richard was in charge of a patrol and he got onto the radio. His "Stick" as it was called, of men were mustered in seventeen minutes, which, when you consider how far apart the isolated farms were, was pretty good going.

Norman and Johnny Travers turned out with a truck mounted with a large machine gun. They followed the same route as Nigel and they too were fired on. One bullet passed through one side of the back of Norman's seat and out of the other. Johnny returned fire but in his hurry failed to get the barrel of the gun up far enough before squeezing off a burst. The result was a string of holes stitched down the side of the truck near his father's shoulder. Poor old Norman was under fire from friend and foe alike. Nigel was laughing about it now but it was wouldn't have been much of a joke at the time. I had and still have tremendous admiration for the people I met then and their pioneer like fighting spirit. It was as well that we didn't know at the time how the tragedy of Zimbabwe would eventually turn out.

5

The Great Zambesi

As usual we were about early the next morning. At 5.40 am
Nigel and I were already down at the barns to finish off those
gaffs. The shark hooks which were at least a quarter of an inch
thick with a gape of four inches, now minus their barbs we
proceeded to fix to some straight gum rods. Taking some thin
wire we whipped the hooks to the shafts most satisfactorily.
When tested, by pulling against the leg of the bench, there was
no movement at all.

Depositing the gaffs into the back of the car we drove to the
site of the new house where we found that the Thatchers had
started work. Some 50 yards from the house the Africans had
erected a structure like a rail fence. The rail had projections at
regular intervals so that it resembled a giant comb. In point of
fact, that is exactly what it was. A continual stream of women
carrying on their heads, bundles of long grass from where they
had been cut, brought them to the site and ran them through
the comb into neat loose bunches that were draped over a series
of wires to dry. Other women and girls were selecting bunches
of grass that had dried and re-combing them into bundles just
like the bundles of reed used by Thatchers in England. These
bundles were taken across to the men working on the roof
where they were laid in place and tapped in firmly on the base
to keep the eves in line. The tool used for the job was a flat
wooden bat shaped implement that would be familiar to most
native East Anglians and anyone else who has watched
Thatchers at work.

With lunch under our belts we loaded the "bakkie", in other
words the Toyota pick up truck and set off for Salisbury and the
home of one of the five Thornycroft sons. This one was Mike
who lived in the city with his then partner Vivian. Mike was a

commercial pilot who at that time was "driving" as his father put it, DC10 freight planes, usually to Schipol, Holland's main airport. Later Mike progressed to 747 Jumbo Freighters and his parents hitched a lift to the UK laying on the floor with a bag of buffalo biltong for a pillow. "A most uncomfortable flight, but at least it got us there". Recalled Nigel. On arrival and after introductions we loaded a canoe and an outboard motor onto the truck. The boat was firmly secured by a couple of Mike's cargo straps, which take up the last of the slack with a lever and clamp system.

Viv's mother, Mrs Saltzmann joined us for supper that evening. A little Jewess who fussed around talking incessantly. When she learned that we were on our way to the Zambesi Valley she threw her hands in the air and thrust her face into mine saying. "Oh my poy, my poy, you must be zo careful of ze crocodiles." I assured her that she need have no worries on that score! Over supper we were comparing the farming in Africa with that in the UK. I heard that the west of Zimbabwe has very little water and was mostly down to cattle ranching. The land is so poor that to run the amount of cattle to make it viable a rancher requires 20,000 – 30,000 acres but, the land was only $Z 15 per acre and $Z1 was then worth £0.75 so, at that time for £23,000 you could buy the necessary land. About a twentieth of the price of a 200-acre farm in Cambridgeshire at the same date.

The conversation then moved to discuss radical changes being made by the new government without enough thought being given to the likely affect of their actions. For example in re-naming Salisbury as Harare it was thought necessary to rename all the streets at the same time. Picture your own town or village – if one, or even two or three streets were re-named the inhabitants would get used to them and be able to cope with further changes. But, if the whole lot were changed overnight no one would know where the devil they were or who lived where. That was Harare in 1981 and just to make things more confusing, people were prematurely removing the old street signs and taking them away as souvenirs.

The area of Mike's house seemed massive and when I awoke in the morning I tried to remember where the bathroom was. Nigel and Corona were sleeping in the guest quarters out in a courtyard and the house was still and quiet as I padded across a large open space with tall windows like the foyer of a substantial hotel. I showered and began to shave when a parrot stalked into the bathroom and began to make a nuisance of itself by taking an interest in my toes. It may have been friendly but we hadn't been introduced and I wasn't taking any chances with bare feet against that formidable bill. I put on my slippers and felt slightly more protected when Viv appeared and picked up the errant Polly. "I've been looking for you." She said. "Mike and I have just taken a cup of tea to his parents. I came to wake you but you beat me to it – coffees in ten minutes."

At 6.00 am we left Salisbury behind and began our journey along the Great North Road. If that conjures up a vision of the A1 think again. The road was good but once away from the town we met about one vehicle every fifty miles – great, this was my kind of motoring! The farther North we travelled so the more evidence there was of the fighting. Burnt out farmhouses and mortared buildings with great holes in the walls. We drove on and on until at last we came to the Sinoa Caves Motel, which was our rendezvous with the rest of our party. Peter Charles "Pip" Thornycroft and his wife Pam were already there and we were not far into a pot of a coffee when a third pick-up arrived. This was Richard with Gerrit von Memerty. Gerry (pronounced with a hard G) as he was called was an old friend of the family and in Nigel's opinion, one of the best and most experienced African big game hunters still living.

We breakfasted at the Motel and then departed in convoy for a further trek via the small towns of Karoi and Makuti, which are about 70 miles apart, to a place called Marangora. At this stage of the journey we began to see baboons wandering about and it began to get noticeably hotter. I found that out when I lent my bare arm on the open window frame and quickly removed it. I smiled at a couple of road signs. One was a warning of Elephants crossing and pictured the silhouette of an

Elephant. Right against it was a temporary road-works sign of a man shovelling a heap of soil. The two together looked as if the man was cleaning up after Jumbo. I wished my camera had been handy.

At Marangora there was just a rather smart building that was the reception station for hunters using the Urungwe game and safari area. We had to call in to register and collect licences. There appeared to be tusks, horns and antlers on every wall and over every door in the place and on the patio outside, the massive skull of a Hippopotamus. Marongora is high on the escarpment above the Zambesi Valley and shortly after leaving it the road bears to the right on the cliff edge giving one the thrilling first sight of the bushveldt far below. Miles and miles of dry, dusty and hot bush, looking as level as the fens spreading to each horizon to right and left. Ahead, some fifty miles away Zambia rose above the valley on its side of the great river. Down, down we went following the winding road to the bottom of the escarpment and then away on the road through the bush to Chirundu on the Zambian border. We saw our first game on the side of this road – a wart hog, which scurried away with its tail comically erect. Of course the purpose of this posture is not to amuse humans, it is so that any of its fellows, particularly its young, can see where it is as they all flee through cover and so keep together. Just before Chirundu we left the main road and taking a dirt track, entered the hunting associations concession area. Near the track was a corrugated iron hut and a barrier used by African rangers from the governments parks & wildlife department. How they could stand the heat in a tin hut I do not know. The interior must have been like an oven. I pondered this as we waited there for the others to catch up. In the distance amid the yellow reeds of the wide flood plains near the river we saw our first elephant and then eight buffalo. A flash of colour in the corner of my eye caused me to turn in time to see some beautiful cinnamon rollers flying past.

The others came up behind us, a quick word, a check to see if the boats were still secure and we made our steady advance along the dusty tracks through the "jesse" (*pronounced jess*) as the scrub is known. The best description of it is that it looks rather like hawthorn scrub, most of it not more than ten feet high, more sparse in some places than others. Trees dotted here and there, but where the jesse was thick the horizon was limited to a few feet either side of the truck. In the more open areas we

Trucking the canoes through the bush

saw game, usually impala as they bounded away at high speed. What I shall always remember though as my real introduction to the game of the valley was a mighty kudu bull when, with his superb spiralled horns flat along his back, he leapt across the track only ten yards ahead of us. The graceful arc of his bound seemed to take him right over the bonnet of the truck. Before we got to our campsite we saw several more kudu, impala and a fish eagle. Among the more unpleasant creatures to make it presence known was the tsetse fly. As soon as we entered the bush we began to be bitten and it was to be a daily torment until we left their domain. They look very like those gad flies or "clegs" that are found around cattle and on cowpats in Britain. Grey – brown, long and speckled. They act in a similar way too – you are not aware of their presence until you are bitten and the pain is sharp. Their bodies are so strong you cannot swat them. You have to swat them and roll them under the palm of your hand. You can feel and hear them crunch. It's too late of course, but it don't half make you feel better – revenge is sweet! The only thing to be said in its favour is that because cattle cannot live where there are tsetse, the fly had saved this and other superb areas of wilderness from human despoliation. In fact Nigel called the tsetse fly Africa's best game warden.

There were three campsites in 500 square miles – **A**, **B** and **C** camps. Ours was **C** camp. They were deliberately spaced many miles apart so that there was little danger of bullets from one lot of hunters reaching anyone else. We began to unload the trucks but Gerry said. "Here Phil. Come and see." I followed him and could see that we were on a low cliff about twenty feet above a narrow beach at the rivers edge. The river stretched away – how far, half a mile wide? More? Less? Distance over water is so difficult to judge. Gerry proudly swept his arm around saying dramatically. "This Phil is the Grreat Zambesi." I felt like a character from Rider-Haggard's *"King Solomon's Mines!"*

We ran the canoe down to the waters edge where I immediately saw my first hippos. I counted 18 in the nearest herd to the camp. I learned later that it was due to hippos that the camp was on the low cliff. Richard pointed out that the massive animals come out at night to graze and they are not over fussy where they tread. The only concession to comfort on these camps site was a building with a toilet, a shower and an open fronted store-cum-shelter in case it rained. The water was pumped up by hand from the river to a large tank. Pip and Pam had brought two of their farm boys, Phineas and Tobias and it was their job to pump the water, collect firewood and butcher any meat brought into the camp. Pip's farm was in the North of the country at Centenary and I noticed that when addressing us his boys used the term Bwana rather than Baas. Two trackers had joined Richard and Gerry at Marangora. Their presence was a condition of the licence and they were to assist the hunter with their unrivalled tracking skills. Their names were Jackson and Takewere and I have no doubt that they were also the eyes and ears of the Parks & Game department.

We dumped most our stores into the shelter along with a battery-powered fridge, which was chokka block full with bottles containing the products of the Castle or Lion breweries, and then set about sorting out our beds. They were those folding canvas covered tubular affairs sold in our garden centres as Sun-loungers. A pillow, a sleeping bag and a mosquito net and the bed was ready. There were more trees along the riverbank and they arched high above us like the inside of a dome. A fire was built and when going well, fed with logs then left to burn down for cooking.

Nigel and I went along the rivers edge to pick out some fishing spots. He said. "Watch out for crocs while I take my ritual swim." So saying, my host stripped off and waded into the river looking not unlike a great white heron. No crocs appeared but I am pretty sure he wasn't relying on my greenhorn eyes for his survival. After his bathe Nigel told me a bit about Gerry. Gerrit von Memerty had once worked for the District Commissioner and part of his job had been to provide meat for the Commissioner's African employees. He became an experienced hunter and something of an expert where elephants were concerned. He had shot over 100 in his career and in that paradoxical way that non-hunters always find so difficult to understand, he loved the great beasts and everything about them. They were his life. Nigel's admiration for Gerrit the man and his expertise comes across in part of the very descriptive letter I will insert here.

Marandellas
18th October 1982

...Had an amusing ten days down the valley. Hot as the hobs of... but tremendous fun and we met with a fair amount of game. Rather an attenuated party - Corona, Richard and I in the main, Gerry von Memerty for four days only and Mike three. A small quota – impala, wart hog, bushbuck, kudu - and those I left for Richard though in fact, I could have taken the lot – no, never got a chance at a bushbuck myself. He covered a lot of mileage and had his share of adventures and in doing so got his impala and bushbuck. Warthog he left as we wanted a half grown one and only met up with grown-ups. Kudu defeated him despite manful efforts. Gerry and I formed an old mans brigade and covered a lot of miles by vehicle, not so many on foot and many hours on our bums waiting and watching. In the event the policy paid dividends; one day we had three kudu browsing in the open within 80 yards for upwards of an hour. Another we spent two hours with a pride of five lions and a lot of lesser stuff. He is an absolute genius with elephant, having shot over 100 and our main ploy was to try and get into any bunch we saw and really get a good look. We must have got to within 30 yards of over twenty bulls and never a one knew it – unless they heard my teeth chattering. One glorious bull – I think the heaviest ivory I have ever seen – we stayed with for probably a quarter of a mile as he ambled through the bush – in four times to within 30 yards. Gerry shaking a small bag of ash at very nearly every stride to test any possible flaw in the wind. In – back – round – in again – muttering each time we got close – The ivory looks better each time – me widdling myself and praying the damn stuff would drop out so that he could really examine it without annoying its legitimate owner. But he was a grand beast. We reckoned his tusk stuck out in front of his trunk a good three feet and must have weighed over 60 lbs a side and a beautifully matched pair.

Once only we might have got into trouble. A patch of very thick jesse – maybe 100 acres and a winding jumble of game tracks like a maze. We heard tummy rumblings in various spots and decided to investigate cautiously. Our tracker decided that discretion was the better part of valour and firmly stayed in the open. I rather wished I had the courage to stay with him – anyway – cautious creeping down game tracks. The damn tummy rumblings now sounded like thunderclaps in all directions and practically on top of us. I knelt for a moment to try and see under a patch. Not 15 yards away a thing like a damn great black worm wriggling. I whistled – we froze and round the bush came a <u>tiny</u> elephant calf, his trunk wriggling and questing inquisitively followed a few yards later by mum, waving her ears to catch what had amused her child. Mercifully the wind held and we beat a <u>very</u> slow and dignified retreat and though suspicious, she never actually picked us up, though she probably heard my sigh of relief when we reached the open. But the tummy rumblings continued from all directions. There must have been quite a bunch in that bit of jesse. Which in fact was encouraging, as they never rumble when alarmed. Some folk consider that they use these rumblings as a form of intimate conversation among themselves. But in itself it is an alarming noise close up. Even Gerry admitted we might not have been very wise going into stuff as thick as that after an unknown number of cows. But as I said, he's an absolute genius with elephant and they are one of his passions in life, and an utter joy to be with alone in the bush, and nowadays, like me, rather un-bloodthirsty apart from food...N.

At dusk on our first night in the bush we all sat along the sand cliff overlooking the river listening to the noises. I say dusk – the sun sank over Zambia and then it was dark, there was no afterglow as we are used to in the UK and it was only about 7.30. The noise of the frogs had to be heard to be believed and later baboons took up the chorus. We sat there enjoying our ration of two cold beers per person per day, until we were watching stars and satellites. With no light pollution the stars were truly visible. Millions of bright twinkling diamonds cushioned on a sky of lush black velvet. We moved back to the fire for supper, which that night was red beans and "sudza" or mealie meal. Made from maize it is a thick substance with a consistency not unlike a cross between porridge and suet dumplings - fairly tasteless, but very filling. It is the Africans staple diet. Traditionally no utensils are used and each one around the fire dipped in to take his or her handful direct from the pot. Gerry commented that the Africans who come on these hunting trips are excited because they know they are going to get fresh meat, which they rarely enjoy at home. They gorge themselves for the first few days but the novelty soon wears off and they are looking for their sudza again.

The moon lit up the river until it shone like a sheet of molten lead, a fact that inspired Gerry and Richard, when supper was over, to take out the canoe and attempt to catch a small crocodile to take home to the farm. They returned after half an hour having had no success. I suppose it was around 8.30 when we all turned in. It was thrilling to lay there in my sleeping bag on that first night under the stars in the bush listening to all the night noises, including the hippos in the river. Their call was a grunt sounding as though they were exhaling and blowing out water followed by a Santa Claus like laugh... "Wooosh! Wumpff, grunt, grunt. Uh!Huh!Huh! Huh!"

My bed was under a lower tree and the two boxes of bait hung on a branch only two feet above my head. I kept feeling something dropping onto my face and realised that the worms were moving around in the boxes and soil was falling from the air holes. I moved my bed aside and resolved to relocate completely in daylight. I settled once more to the sound of baboons rustling about in the treetops not far away.

Our camp - Zambesi Valley 1981

6

Life in the Bushveldt

By dawn the baboons had moved across into the trees directly above us. I lay on my bed watching them cavorting about and shouting to one another. The trees were tamarind trees and the baboons were eating the beans that are the fruit of the tree. The discarded husks of the beans were dropping down onto us but it could have been worse! I picked up a husk and was idly inspecting it when Gerry appeared and told me that it was believed that this species of tree had been introduced by seed/beans dropped by Arab slavers raiding in the area years ago.

The fire was revived enough to make coffee for breakfast after which Gerry, Pip and Takewere went off in a truck to search for kudu. Richard, Corona and Pam took the canoe out while Nigel and I tried the shore for tiger fish. We worked along the shore for a quarter of a mile when we came to a backwater, which we tried for a barbel or a bream. Nigel took a barbel, which turned out to be our sole catch. The birds were taking most of my attention, all kinds of birds all new to me and identified by my host. Red-billed teal, white winged plover, two vultures, and a fish eagle. In the cliff face were three colonies of carmine bee-eaters – 600 nest holes in each colony. There were lesser and white fronted bee-eaters too, but the carmines were by far the most numerous in this spot. I was delighted to see a pair of stilts, wading on very long legs. A bird I had always wanted to see in England. I was not to know then that that ambition would be fulfilled two years later.

We regained the cliff top and wandered along the edge towards the end of the backwater. There was a sandy beach there and on it were 100 impala, some of the rams sparring and beyond them a wart hog and several baboons could be seen scavenging about. They saw us and in an instant the beach was just bare sand. Between the cliff edge and the trees we came across a huge splash of blood surrounded by gory blobs and streaks. Very obviously something had met with a violent end during the night. Nigel quietly inspected it and after a moment said. "Perhaps this is as good a time as any to remind you that you are in dangerous game country. Most things will go quietly away if you stand still, but it's if you come across say a lioness, so suddenly that she feels cornered is when it can be dangerous. The thing is to keep your eyes open ahead of you and try not to walk into any trouble."

It was clear that at times of high water the bank between the backwater and the river would become an island but on this day we were able to walk over the beach to the river where we found a number of hippos and crocodiles. One ten-foot long croc launched itself from the bank right under our noses. Walking back we saw giant and pied kingfishers, two-spot dove and an Egyptian goose. Some hornbills, strange looking with their great "Guinness advertisement" bills and on some damp patches, clouds of beautiful green and yellow swallowtail butterflies. There were enormous anthills dotted all over the place. Some of four-foot diameter and ten feet tall, others shorter and wider, all weird and wonderful shapes.

The camp was quiet during the siesta of midday but later Pam took me along the river edge to where she had found the decomposing body of a large croc. I stepped it out at 14 feet and then knocked some teeth out of the stinking carcass to take back as souvenirs. In the mud and sand near and just away from the river we founds tracks of elephant, hippo, lion, rhino, waterbuck and buffalo.

An hour before dusk Gerry invited me to accompany him and the two trackers in a hunt for guinea fowl for the pot. At first we drove through the bush in one of the trucks and passed a couple of buffalo standing in a clump of trees. The trackers who were riding in the body of the truck were keeping their eyes open from their higher vantage point. Suddenly there came a tap on the cab roof. Jackson was pointing to the thick vegetation ahead. Gerry pulled up and we disembarked. Gerry with a 12 bore at the ready. I couldn't see anything but then up went the gun and the first guinea was in the bag – shot on the ground. On again until we found some more. Same procedure – Bang! On the ground. Then all hell let loose as a dozen or more erupted like so many turkeys – all around us, unmissible targets, but no shot saluted them. "Why didn't you take one with the second barrel?" I asked. "I am vaiting for ze bastards to come down!" grinned the jovial pole. To my surprise they did. Gerry was a rifleman, not a shotgun shooter and moreover this wasn't sport, it was for the pot. He wasn't going to waste cartridges or risk wounding a guinea and have to follow it up. It made sense when I thought it over but it did seem strange at the time.

While we were driving back to camp Gerry noticed that I had lost the index finger of my left hand and asked about it. I told him how I had shot it off when carelessly climbing a gate with a loaded gun. He laughed and then held up his own left hand, which also had the index finger missing. Naturally, I wanted to know the history of that. The story was that he had developed a knack of picking up snakes, even the most poisonous species and thought himself quite an expert. One night he was having a drink when someone came in and advised everyone to be careful because there was a puff adder on the road just outside the club. Gerry said. "Oh I'll soon get rid of him." However, the drink he had consumed caused an error of judgement and the snake was too quick for him. The finger had to be quickly amputated to prevent the deadly poison getting into his system. Then I found out that Nigel had also lost a finger – his due to getting chemical spray into a bad barbed wire cut. We tried to work out the odds against three out of five men in a party of seven all having a finger missing. We gave up, but what a coincidence – perhaps we should have formed an elite club?

We were laughing about this over supper when, from the Zambian side of the river, came the sound of African drums. Not just from one spot but from one village to another. There was some discussion as to whether or not the drums were used as some kind of primitive telegraph. Gerry was of the opinion that they were not. He said that over the years he had met some very experienced people in the ways of the African and although simple signals would be possible, he had never met any one Black or White, who could "read the drums" Pip said "Well, it is Saturday night, they're probably just calling all the neighbours to the local hop. – after all, most of them have got transistor radios now." Whatever the purpose of the drums, for me they did add that little extra to the exciting atmosphere.

Sunday 18th October. Being a knowledgeable naturalist and knowing that I was interested, Corona took me a little way from camp to show me a kygelia tree also known as the german sausage tree because of its strange fruit. This particular tree was fairly hanging with what certainly looked like foot long sausages of about four inches in diameter. Corona informed me that it has been found that if sliced like a cucumber the juices are very beneficial if rubbed onto skin cancer. She also said that the native Africans had been aware of the fruit's health giving properties for years and had long known it as good "muti" (*medicine*)

Another tree that interested me throughout my stay in the bush was the great baobab. The legend is that god got angry with the tree and stuck it headfirst into the ground. The branches really do resemble large roots. The wood is soft and is often damaged by elephants. Some baobabs are massive with girths of several feet, indeed there are one or two in places nearer to civilization where people have hollowed out the bottom of the trunk and fitted them out with tables and chairs. On the whole I think I preferred to see them as nature intended.

Corona, Pip and I took the rods and canoe up river and moored off some rocks spending an hour or so spinning for tiger fish. It wasn't very productive; our catch was a chesser for me and a tiger for Pip. We saw a crocodile sweeping along below us - a sinister submariner. New birds for my list - crowned plover, green backed heron, an osprey, trumpeter hornbills, and lanner falcon. We landed on the rocks and found the nest and two eggs of a pair of pratincoles. From there we could see along the rivers edge and not far away was a goliath heron, a monster bird, which stands six feet tall.

We took Corona back to the camp and were joined by Nigel. This time we paddled downstream until we came to some rapids. Leaving the canoe we fished from the rocks in the turbulent waters. Tiger fish were coming through and some took an interest in our flashing spinners. Once Pip and I struck into fish at the same time and he shouted to Nigel to get one too, so that we all had one. Incredibly he did just that and then Pip lost his. They were not big for tigers, ours averaged 3-4 pounds, but like pike, they get a lot bigger than that. They fight like pike too – we certainly knew when we'd got one on. Even I the novice bagged two, Nigel 3 and Pip 2 and a bream. They were big enough to eat and as we were living on what we caught, more than welcome.

As we paddled home we came across some Zambians waist deep in the river putting out nets. They did not appear to be over worried by the presence of crocs. Others paddled dugout canoes and yet another strode along the bank with a leash of red-billed teal, which he must have snared somehow. They grinned and waved as we passed – fellow hunters. They had their supper – we were heading in the direction of ours which tonight turned out to be smoked barbel and tiger fish with the usual sudza. Our meal was once again eaten to the accompaniment of the Zambian drummers. Tonk! Tonka! Tonka! Tonk!..

Later a breeze built up to a strong wind, which heralded a storm. Spectacular sheet lightning periodically illuminated distant mountains, but there was very little in the way of rain. There was suddenly a devil of a racket when a baboon must have been blown out of his tree.

Monday 19th October. I have always been a morning person but I don't think I have ever felt better than when, on this camp we used natures timepiece for sleeping and rising. The light woke me and as I lay on my bed for a few moments each morning, as regular as clockwork the call of a fish eagle came to the ears.

"Coooy! Coy! Coy! Coy!" he cried as he hunted along the river for his breakfast. A large dark bird with a white head and neck he swept majestically over the camp.

I had just finished washing and shaving when Richard and Gerry came back in with a bushbuck that Richard had shot at first light. The boys set about butchering the little beast. After rustling up some breakfast Corona, Pam, Richard and I took a truck through the bush to **B** Camp. Pam and I were in the open truck and the tsetse flies were in a murderous mood. Through the back window of the cab Richard was laughing at our arm flailing attempts to ward them off, By the end of the ten mile journey we must have received 200 bites each and by that time the joke was wearing thin. However, we managed to see five wart hog and a couple of elephants between bouts with the fly. The elephant was a cow with a large calf. They lumbered up a slope into the cover of the trees as the truck rattled and lurched past within seventy yards.

B camp was situated on a beautiful wide horseshoe bend in the river with high, forested hills beyond. Spreading out, we set up our tackle and fished. I hooked and landed a tiger fish almost at once, but it proved to be my only fish. An African, standing erect in a primitive dugout canoe appeared drifting round the bend, cast – netting as he went. I had never seen anyone using a cast-net before and it was fascinating to see him arrange the net and weights carefully over one arm and with a smooth swinging movement send it to splash in a perfect circle a few yards from him. A fish eagle and an osprey flew by while the boat was still in view – all fishermen together in their own way. We too, and we had modern equipment on our side but my guess is that we were the least successful of them all.

Pam was not fishing and had opted to act as cook girl. She soon had a small fire going within a ring of stones. I had moved along to some rapids where I lost another tiger and two more spinners that snagged in the rocks. I packed up before I lost too much of the Thornycroft's tackle. I joined Pam and while we enjoyed a fresh brew of tea she told me how they came to buy their farm. Pip had worked for the owners and at the start of the troubles had come home one day to find the couple lying murdered in the road near their house. When everything had been sorted out, Pip had been able to purchase the farm from the beneficiaries of the will. They had made precautions against visits from terrorists and the children knew that at the first sign of trouble they were to get into a pre-arranged secret hiding place inside the house. Apparently Pip was out one night when someone tried to get into the wired off compound. The children followed their drill and Pam fired blindly out of the windows. The intruders decided the fire was too hot and departed into the darkness.

The others joined us for tea and then scrambled eggs, followed by canned grapefruit chunks all eaten out of the same cups! It may sound messy but lord it was good. It was getting hotter and that grapefruit was a lifesaver. While we lay on the bank first a martial eagle and then a crowned eagle flapped overhead on heavy wings. Corona had caught just one N'kupi, but Richard had got among 'em and had a brace of barbel and some tiger. For the drive back to C camp Richard volunteered to take his share of the tsetse attack. He wrapped an old blanket around him, which at least gave some protection.

During the heat of midday we all lounged about reading or dozing, or in my case, keeping up my diary. After a couple of hours I wandered off on my own to the backwater, hiding at the base of the cliff to see what turned up. Two pied kingfishers began diving and splashing about, then five stilts flew past, long, long legs trailing behind them. A single lesser bee-eater pitched on the cliff top not far away and a fish eagle banked in mid-flight to glide down into a tree overlooking the main river. Then a most extraordinary bird appeared. Like a giant tern, but as it glided past twenty yards in front of my hiding place it dropped its lower mandible vertically down and with it, ploughed the surface of the water. I guessed that the idea was to catch any surface feeding fish but as to what it was I hadn't a clue. "African Skimmer". Said Nigel, when I later described the bird to him. "You lucky so and so, I can't remember seeing one down here myself." That information came later though and for the moment I had other things to occupy my thoughts. Four waterbuck, three hinds and a buck came down to the waters edge but they were uneasy and immediately turned back to scramble up the cliff. The buck stopped, his forefeet higher than his heels, and stared right at me. He couldn't see me but sensed something was different and faded ghostlike into the bush where even the striking white ring on his rump just vanished.

My next visitors were thirteen guinea fowl all black; light blue and speckled with white. Pity about their ugly heads. They stalked about like hens round a stack yard. I was watching them and a blacksmith plover that had dropped in to wade about in the shallows when three waterbuck came down off the island to join a bushbuck on the dusty "beach" where the backwater petered out. A second bushbuck turned up and took its mate away into cover. One by one the waterbuck lay down. I watched them for half an hour and in that time decided that would be good to move back into cover and stalk them through the jesse. Interesting plan, but as soon as I moved – oh so slowly – even though they were 500 yards away, they saw me and stood up. The next second there was nothing there at all but a puff of yellow dust drifting away on a slight breeze. I stood upright now, cramped after crouching so still. I stretched and ambled to a spot on the cliff where there was a colony of carmine bee-eaters. A good 600 nest holes were bored into the face of the cliff and a mass of the vivid deep pink of the owners of the nests whirled and flashed as hundreds of birds came and went in endless movement. I sat with my legs dangling over the edge with nest holes either side, the nearest within arms length and these beautiful creatures went about their business as though I didn't exist. On this trip I saw so many new birds and beasts that it is difficult to pick out any one above another, but this little episode certainly is one of the first I remember whenever I think about the Zambesi Valley.

Back at camp Richard took me to one side to tell me of a plan to get me a shot at guinea fowl. As a non-hunting guest it was not really allowed but Nigel was keen that I should put up a gun at least once while in the Valley. The plan was that when we got into the bush Gerry would lead off <u>both</u> trackers leaving Richard and I alone and giving me my opportunity. Alas, we got a puncture on the way out and that was the end of that little venture. Richard did manage to bag a guinea as we made our way back so the larder was replenished.

Sunset, with our cold beers as usual as we sat in a line along the bank listening to the frogs and hippos… and the drums. We went over the events of the day and when we swore about the morning's mass attack by the tsetse Nigel said. "Oh, you don't want to worry about that, only 1 fly in 20,000 carries the sleeping sickness!" The ritual of sundowners over we returned to our places around the campfire and enjoyed the results of Richard's early morning hunt – pot-roasted bushbuck, sudza, red beans and mouth-watering bushbuck steaks. Our mouths were not alone in watering. With meat in camp we attracted our first visit from hyenas. Most of the bushbuck had been cut into small strips of meat and hung on paper clip hooks on a special little building purpose built for the job. There are many racks where the meat hangs drying to become biltong. The American Red Indians call it pemmican. Naturally the scent of all this meat wafts through the bush in a very inviting fashion. The biltong racks are built high out of the reach of scavengers.

The baboons as usual were noisily making the own preparations for sleep high up in the trees around and above us. Occasionally twigs would drop onto us and everyone was mildly cursing them. I suggested firing a 12 bore into trees to clear them off. Gerry grinned and said. "Ah! That's a thing you only do once Phil. I tried it once and I soon discovered that baboons have very slack bowels!"

Later in the evening we had turned in and lay listening to the various night noises when a new sound, new to me at least, was heard. At a distance at first, a long drawn out howl, gradually getting closer until it was not far from the camp. Ahooooooa! Arooooooa! "What the hell is that?" I muttered. Nigel's voice replied from somewhere beyond the still flickering fire. "Hyenas. They can smell the meat. We'll start having bigger fires now those bastards are about." For reasons best known to themselves the hyenas did not come in to the camp that night but I shall long remember their weird introduction to my experience of life.

It was the practice of Gerry at camp to set up his bed some distance away from other people. Whether it was for privacy or that he relished the feeling of solitude and intimacy with the wild I never found out, but it led him into some narrow scrapes. Perhaps it was the buzz he got from that. On this particular night two elephants had walked along the edge of camp right by Gerry's bed. The footprints seen the next morning were clear as day. Just under two years after this camp Gerry was not so lucky. A lion – probably startled by his snoring as it padded past gave him a swat with its paw before fleeing. Our hero's face was badly injured and had to be repaired with sixty-six stitches. The full story is detailed in a letter printed in chapter 9.

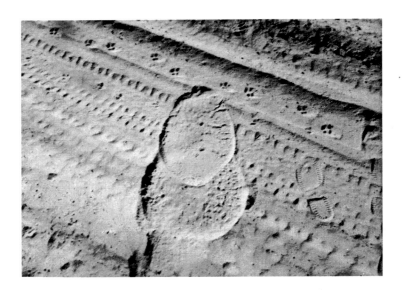

Elephant spoor - and a mans' to compare.

7

Tsetse flies and mopane bees

Tuesday 20th October 1981. Richard and Gerry departed early on this morning, as they had to return to their respective farms. At 7.00 am Nigel, Pip and I with the two trackers drove 15 to 20 miles through the bush to the Sharu River. At this time of the year the Sharu is dry, the riverbed looking like a rough stony road. We left the truck and split up. Pip went off with Takewere and they were very soon lost from view in the thick cover. Nigel and I moved away in another direction with Jackson our tracker. Jackson wore the green hat and boiler suit of the Game & Wildlife Department and carried a military rifle. I noticed that both trackers kept a piece of rag in the muzzle of their rifles to keep out dust, twigs or other foreign bodies.

We re-crossed the Sharu and walked slowly along the yellow reed fringes in extended single file following its meandering course towards the Zambesi. During the night, especially in the dry season, all kinds of creatures travel down to the river to relieve their thirst. Most have moved miles back into the bush soon after daybreak but the hope was that some of the smaller stuff was still hanging around. The bed of the little river gradually widened as we came to the spot where it in wetter times, its waters would rush out into the main river. Our way was along the right hand bank of the Sharu and on that side we were still in cover, which was now about to change to tall tawny grasses. Jackson, in mid-stride, froze like a statue as he whispered. "Simba Baas!" 200 yards along the shore stood a lion. He had seen or winded us at once and stood gazing steadily in our direction. His great mane was, because of constant contact with thorny scrub, somewhat shorter than those of his brothers who live in open country. If a camera could have been brought to bear he would have made a good picture but we moved not a muscle. After the lion decided he had seen enough he ambled off into the jesse. We went up to the spot where he had been standing so that I could see his pug marks in the firm sand.

Keeping to the shore for a few miles we re-entered the jesse. The wind was now in our favour and we worked our way back into it. Scores of impala bounded away, the last ones leaping mightily to overtake their neighbours and escape the vulnerable position at the rear. This caused the new rearguard to panic and make its own leap. I saw this spectacle many times during this short spell in the bush, but it never failed to hold me captivated. I found the skull and horns of an impala and carried it as an intended souvenir but sometime during the morning I put it down for a moment and forgot to pick it up.

Waterbuck, bushbuck and warthog all scurried away as we approached and with much crashing and thumping two buffalo thundered off. I began to wonder how anything could be approached at all with all the noise we were causing. Most things were spotting us well before we saw them. In fact it was often only through the sound of their flight that I saw them at all. Regularly, as we came across droppings, Nigel would tell me from which beast they come and, in the case of the antelopes, he would squeeze it between finger and thumb to ascertain how far we were behind its maker.

In a clearing we came across striped mongoose. Six of the little creatures were playing among some fallen timber. They appeared to be having a whale of a time tumbling about, chasing and jumping and squeaking at each other completely ignoring us. A small thrush sized falcon sped by through the low branches and in a brief window of sky two vultures and an eagle hove into view together. We did come across the kudu we were after but not close enough for a shot. They are so very hard to see if they keep still and it was only when one moved its ears to shake off a fly that Nigel picked it up and pointed it out by means of whispered directions.

Suddenly, or so it seemed to me who hadn't a clue where I was, we hit the Sharu river again and followed it back to the rendezvous. The truck was not there, in its place was an orange under which was a note from Pip. It read:

Pa,

    Have collected a rather large bull and am attempting to drive the truck up the far side of the Sharu.

    Its about 2 miles up river and 200 yards from the river, on the left bank looking upstream.

    All being well we will be back here within the hour.

      10.40 now.

We split the orange three ways and sat down for a breather while Nigel told me of other hunts he had enjoyed. Less than an hour had passed when we picked up the first sounds of the approaching truck and before long it appeared bucking and rolling over the rough ground. I peeped into the back of the vehicle. Pip had his kudu bull all right, a fine looking beast with horns three feet six inches long.

We passed round a plastic container of foul tasting warm water. It certainly wasn't nectar but it lubricated parched throats in readiness for the long drive back to camp.

The boys, supervised by Pip, set about gralloching and butchering the kudu as soon as we could get it unloaded and hoisted up from a stout branch of a tree. As with Richard's bushbuck most of it was cut into strips and hung up to dry into biltong. In the then recent fighting the Rhodesian soldiers carried biltong in their packs as an easy, ready to eat meal. Speaking of matters military reminds me that as we walked along the rivers edge I found an FN cartridge case.

After a snack lunch and a decent interval Corona, Pip and I took the canoe down to the rapids. It was windy, so it was a rough and very wet ride – but at least the water was warm! We saw three crocodile and a goliath heron and on the rocks near the rapids, a baby pratincole in the nest we found recently. We fished gamely but the tigers were not playing. A fish eagle soared over and probably viewed our efforts with contempt. Pam waved as she walked along the shore to get nearer to a herd of forty hippos, which were grunting and splashing a quarter of a mile downstream. It was about then that Pip got into the only fish of the day. When Nigel had been briefing me as to what to expect from the fishing he had talked of tiger fish, bream and vundu, as the fish he hoped would provide our sport. Vundu he had explained was a giant barbel, which could tip the scale at over 80 lbs. There had been reports, he added, of large ones taking African children as they waded in the river. The usual bait for these monsters was, of all things, blue soap. I was to use some myself later. It looked like Danish blue cheese – white, flecked with blue. The attraction must have been the pungent smell, as I cannot think it would have had an appetizing taste. Anyway, back to the rapids. Pip's rod was bent double and quivering like the tail of an excited spaniel on the first day of the shooting season. He played it carefully, gradually working into a gap in the rocks. "Get ready with the gaff Phil!" he shouted. Our shark hook gaffs were coming into their own after all. Pip steadily drew the fish, I could see it now, up within reach and I carefully gaffed it under the chin and hauled it onto the rocks. An ugly looking brute of 30 – 40 lbs, so a tiddler! Pip asked me to knock it on the head. I picked up the nearest large stone and brought it down sharply. The stone broke in two. It was only sandstone but it was hard enough. I looked up and my face must have been a picture of amazement for Pip laughed and said. "Hard skull isn't it?" He then killed the great fish by cutting through it's vertebrae and we headed back to camp while the vundu was at it's freshest.

The boys had been instructed to collect dead branches of mopane trees because evidently the wood burns a long time and from now on, because of the hyenas, we wanted to keep a big fire burning all night without having to keep feeding it. That night the fire was big and the light thrown back by the tree canopy high above gave the impression of being inside a huge dome. The supper was kudu liver with onions and was most excellent fare. Stories were related as we drew back from the heat of the fire.

Nigel told of one camp in the Valley when they had all dropped off to sleep and were abruptly startled into wakefulness by terrible screams. It turned out that two of the boys, who cook and sleep perhaps 100 yards from the main camp, had unbeknown to each other, both found the need to relieve themselves and had crept off into the darkness. They had somehow backed into each other and both were convinced that they had been grabbed by some ferocious beast. It should be remembered that most Africans live on farms or townships and some never see their own big game in their lifetime. So it is easy to understand how the imaginations of these two boys ran wild on the night in question.

That night was pretty eventful in it's own right. The hyenas came attracted by even more biltong. Howling weirdly, like ghouls on Halloween and then chuckling horribly, invisible outside the light of the fire. They wanted to get to the meat, but they weren't brave enough - yet. Later, when the baboons had settled and silence reigned over the camp all hell was let loose.

Screams, barks, and crashes as the baboon colony erupted in all directions. Corona's voice came out of the darkness. she said that she had heard a leopard cough moments before and thought it had either taken one or got in among the colony and put the fear of god into them. To cap that, while we were all asleep, Pam saw two elephants pass along the cliff edge within twenty yards of our beds. In the morning we could see the spoor and a flattened bush behind my bed. "How the devil did you sleep through that?" they all laughed. I wished that I had been awake.

Wednesday 21ˢᵗ October 1981. Nigel and Pip drove out at daybreak to try for kudu again. I spent a lazy morning along the backwater and the island. There were some hippos lounging in the river just off the island and by creeping in behind some bushes I was able to get close enough for a decent photograph. As I scrambled to get up I peered over the cliff top and there just below me lay a two-foot long leguaan. These big lizards raid the bee-eater's nests, crawling into the holes to eat the eggs, chicks or even adults given the chance.

Sitting by the side of the backwater I could see barbel swimming about not far below the surface and then a small face poked out of the water and another and another. Small turtles or terrapins, I don't know which. I am not sure whether they were really looking to see what this strange creature was up to on their riverbank, but it certainly seemed that way. All the birds that I had become used to seeing kept me entertained, including four stilts. I was really pleased to get so many sightings of this wader that is so very rare in Britain.

Back to the camp for a ploughman's lunch and a refreshing jug of lemon tea. Pam was sun bathing on the sandy bank of the river so, after a while Corona and I wandered off with some sea rods and reels to try to tempt a vundu. The blue soap is moulded like putty around ones hook until it resembles a dried out dog turd and surprisingly it stays on. Well, let's say it stays on for several casts. I noticed that little flies were becoming a nuisance by hovering around ones eyes. Corona explained that they were mopane bees and they were attempting to drink the salt from our tear ducts. She said they were harmless but could be trying. We stuck at our casting for an hour or more until Corona commented on the poor fishing this trip. Ten minutes later a vundu was testing her skill and her rod. The rod was up to the task and there was no question about my friend's skill. Eventually, the leviathan was beached and carried triumphantly into camp where I photographed both fish and captor in traditional pose.

Nigel and Pip returned having obtained no reasonable opportunity, but full of stories of what they had seen. They went through their day for us while we enjoyed kudu fillets and a few bottles of wine. The roar of a lion came to us on the still air though I had to agree with Nigel when he said. "I don't know why we call it roaring, it always sounds more like a cow with belly ache to me!" When I thought of the low drawn out moaning one hears from a threatening bull, I had to admit that there was more than a similarity. Perhaps it was insulting to the lion and anyway, I was pleased enough to have heard the voice of the so-called king of beasts at least once in the wild.

The now nightly visit from the hyenas was heralded by the first distant howls. We listened as they relentlessly moved in and when they got into the camp area, to the change from howls to hideous human sounding chuckles. We thought that they were getting rather too near to the meat. They were certainly much nearer than they had dared to venture before. Armed with torches, Pip and I rushed round behind the shelter to where the biltong racks were and shone our beams all about. Between the trees a ring of perhaps forty pairs of eyes reflected back the light of our torches. No shapes, just formless inky darkness and all these pinpoints of bright, sinister light. The baboons up above registered their disapproval at their disturbed night so we retreated to our beds to a chorus of Waahoo! and Oof! Oooof!

The torches and perhaps the large fire appeared to have the desired effect and put the hyenas off. I had hardly turned over in my sleeping bag listening to the hippos conversation from the river when elephants began crashing around amid the trees.

They were not that far away but they did not come near the camp and I drifted off to sleep.

The following morning *Thursday 22nd October 1981,* Nigel and I drove to Chirundu for stores and to collect three repaired tyres that had been taken in by Richard on his way home. Pip and Takewere came with us for part of the way until we dropped them off in the bush for a hunt. A few miles further on we stopped ourselves and tried to stalk four kudu. As Nigel said, in this country you really haven't a hope unless you spot the beast before he spots you – and that's not very often. We were walking quietly along a narrow track through the jesse when we had the most marvellous spectacle of over 400 buffalo crossing the track ahead of us. They took fully five minutes to all get over – a mass of solid black heaving bodies, dust and horns. One or two looked our way, heads back looking over their nostrils, trying to wind us. As the buffalo is probably the only animal in Africa that will go out of its way to try and kill you, I was rather glad that the wind was in our favour! It really was a splendid sight though, whatever the nature of the beast.

Thoughts of the nature of the beast reminds me of an incident involving a buffalo. When Nigel and Corona had not been in Rhodesia that long they were walking steadily, some distance apart though the bush, armed only with shotguns as they were after small game, guinea fowl and such. Suddenly Nigel came across a buffalo bull, which charged. There was nowhere to go, all he could do was fling his arms and legs around the beast's neck and hang on for dear life while it tried to dislodge him. Corona heard the commotion and hurried over to find the buffalo throwing its head around in an attempt to pound her husband onto the ground. Undergoing such treatment he would have soon tired, dropped off and been killed had he been alone. Luckily he wasn't and his plucky wife strode to the beast and fired both barrels into its side from very close range. This caused the buffalo to stagger back where upon Nigel snatched the gun and reloaded just before the animal gathered itself to charge again. I can remember Nigel telling me that he would fire causing the buff to stagger, quickly reload as it came again and repeat the performance. It took something like fifteen shots

before the buffalo finally succumbed and keeled over, leaving them both wobbly with shock and Nigel nursing two broken ribs and plenty of cuts, grazes and bruises. "It was a nasty, messy business," he said. "But it was him or us and we got off very lightly indeed." I doubt if there are many people who have come to such close quarters with an African buffalo and survived to tell the tale.

But, we will return to the somewhat gentler occasion of our walk. We saw Buffalo (*Sociable*) Weavers nests, reputed to all face West and therefore a useful navigation aid. Buitlaars eagle, the inevitable impala and bushbuck, two lots of four bush pigs. A civet – like a black otter cum badger. Two vultures and some vervet monkeys. Nigel pointed out elephant damage to trees especially the huge soft barked baobabs, where the tusks had gouged out great chunks and strips of wood. It was already getting very hot and the tsetse were as usual, a damned nuisance. I crunched and rolled several under my palm but always after they had got the first blow in. While we were standing in a clearing I noticed, not for the first time, an almost continuous rattling sound. When I commented on it Nigel identified the musicians. "Cicada beetles. The sound is produced by two drum like organs in their abdomen."

Driving temporarily out of the bush into the little border outpost we completed our original tasks and came across Pip again at the Chirundu river on the return journey. He had not taken a shot but he had seen another herd of 300 buffs. According to my friends the buffalo population was increasing nicely. We were getting hungry and were more than pleased to arrive back at camp in time for a brunch of beautiful African bream, hard-boiled eggs and rye biscuits. I remember saying that I wished our UK bream were as delicious as those breakfast fish. They tasted as good as plaice and simply melted in the mouth.

Nigel enjoys a quiet pipe

Everyone was lounging about even after a lengthy siesta so I wandered off into the jesse behind the camp for a couple of miles or so. I was already beginning to be able to identify most birds and beasts and even some of the tracks. I saw all the usual stuff and made out the spoor of lion, buffalo and rhino. I would

86

have loved to have seen a rhino but that was not to be. They were certainly about and Pip had warned me. "If you hear a noise like a puffing steam engine behind you, get round the back of the nearest tree, and then, if you have time, get up it!" After a while I came to a spot where I was on the fringes of a troop of baboons. I was watching them when one baby swinging in a tree urinated on another immediately below it. The victim screeched in obvious rage and chased the baby for a short distance. I was engrossed in their antics and suddenly sensed that I too was being watched. I looked up and caught the eye of a big male who stared on unblinkingly. Whether or not he considered me a threat, I felt that he was weighing up the situation and as I was two miles from camp with only a stick in my hands and he had four-inch fangs I decided to back off and leave them to their piece of ground.

That night the hyenas were really noisy and becoming more bold. In the morning we found that they had succeeded in stealing some biltong.

Friday 23ʳᵈ October 1981. Early this morning we loaded the canoe onto the truck and drove the twenty or thirty miles to **A** camp. During the tsetse infested journey along with all the usual birds and beasts, our paths crossed with four elephants and thirty buffalo. We had stopped to watch the latter when a Land Rover appeared out of the bush and pulled up beside the truck. The vehicle was driven by a young white warden of the Game Association, who said that he had just come from **A** camp where some work was being carried out.

A camp is situated at the point where the Zambesi enters the kariba gorge. An hour by boat through the gorge would bring you to kariba dam and beyond to the great lake of the same name. We however, were planning to travel in the other direction - upriver, back to our camp by boat. At **A** we met one Owen Lewis, a member of the Hunter's Association who was supervising a gang of Zulus in the building of some new camp shelters and biltong racks. After we had been shown the work achieved so far we were invited into his tent for a cup of tea.

87

This most English of drinks was more than welcome and did a grand job of washing down the red dust from the tracks through the bush.

Bidding Mr Lewis "Good Morning" we off loaded the canoe and Nigel drove away in the truck to try a bit of hunting on his own account, leaving the rest of us to make our own way back. C camp was perhaps twenty miles away by river and it took us five hours – from 10.00 am to 3.00 pm. To say that Corona, Pam, Pip and I had plenty of room gives an idea as to the size of the canoe and we did have an outboard engine.

As I have discovered on my native East Anglian waterways, travelling by boat, especially a small, low craft gives one a completely different perspective on ones surroundings. Slipping silently along mid-stream of the wide river with sandy cliffs, beaches and islets was quite an experience. Right from the very start we were dodging hippos. The hippopotamus is a harmless looking beast, which in fact annually kills more people than any other animal in Africa. In the beasts defence I must add that it usually the fault of the humans who either get in the hippos path, or appear to be a threat to her offspring. Pip, who was steering the boat, asked us to keep a good look out ahead. Dry rocks showing above the water were probably just rocks, but wet, shiny "rocks" were likely to be the heads of recently surfaced hippo. As soon as we spotted any, which was often, we steered nearer the bank to give them a wide berth. Pip said that if by ill luck a hippo came up from under us and overturned us, we were to get away from the boat as quickly as possible for the angered beast would attack the biggest thing it could see. At this point I reflected once again that I cannot swim, but as each time we took avoiding action and approached the shore great crocodiles, disturbed by our passing, launched themselves from the bank were they had been loafing I thought perhaps I would have to run across top of the waves like some crazy cartoon character to stand a chance of survival. One mean looking creature about fourteen feet long, gave us a really good view as it glided right under the canoe not three feet below our keel.

The song goes – "Never smile at a crocodile." Well, I can assure you that that reptile was certainly not smiling.

Almost inevitably, fish eagles were abundant and we passed a glorious colony of carmine bee-eaters. From time to time at likely looking bays or inlets we set up our rods but it was now very hot and the fishing was poor. Corona landed a squeaker. I don't know if that is the correct name. Somehow I doubt it. It appeared to be a very small shark, but only twelve inches long.

We were moored near a narrow but deep creek when Corona provided the entertainment again. She decided that it would be good to take a cooling dip, so we put her ashore whereupon she dived, fully clothed into the creek. She surfaced choking with laughter. The pressure of her dive through the water had forced her knickers clean off. We all joined in the merriment as she tried to retrieve them.

On again, dodging hippos, we must have passed over 400 in the course of our voyage. An Egyptian goose shepherded her brood of goslings up the bank side as she spotted our approach and on rounding a bend we found an elephant standing on a sandbank spraying water over its back with its trunk. There were a number of sandbanks forming islets on this reach of the river so we selected a largish one of our own, as far out from the shore as we could find and beaching the boat, proceeded to enjoy a picnic in the middle of the Zambesi. The novelty of it was good, but by the time our lunch was over the heat, reflected back up from the sand, was becoming almost unbearable. I soon discovered that the heat was having an effect elsewhere. Knowing from experience that anything that goes in a boat can get wet or suffer knocks of one sort or another, I had brought a small, cheap camera along and slipped it inside my shirt. I had reckoned without the sun – the back of the camera had expanded and buckled in the heat, rendering it useless. Luckily I had my best camera back at the camp, but I lost all my film of the river journey. Once we were on the move again it was slightly cooler as I suppose we created our own breeze. As we drew closer to the shore on a hippo avoidance tack, several turtles popped up to see what was going on. Not far away a great white egret stalked about. I wondered whether or not it would take turtles if it came across them. A proper island, rather than a sandbank hove up ahead. On it could be seen nine black storks. "Woolly necked storks." Put in Corona, pre-empting my query. Then we were passing **B** camp and all too soon we were back to base after an unforgettable voyage along the great Zambesi.

Sprawled around the fire of blazing mopane logs we exchanged stories of our day with Nigel and his hunting foray. He had covered a fair bit of ground but had not had the opportunity of a shot. As he said, it's a lot like wildfowling – it's not the killing that counts, it's the magic of being in the wild and being part of it. Before we turned in Pip and I decided to have a some fun by setting a trap for the marauding hyenas that were expected before too long. Taking a heavy cooking pot we hoisted it up a tree and anchored it with a sensitive slipknot baited with biltong. Phineas the cook – boy was with us and giggled as I imitated a hyena with a headache.

Lying on our beds fully dressed, we waited for the howling band of robbers to make an entrance. We had not long to wait and we could hear them moving outside of the light of the fire. Then - Clang! Went the pot. Pip and I were there in seconds but all we could see was the fallen pot and the now familiar pin points of light from many pairs of wicked looking eyes glaring at us from between the trees. We reset the trap and before long came the clang followed by irritated chattering as the mob scattered once more in panic. This time we had settled into our sleeping bags and didn't bother to investigate.

The heat of the day seemed hardly to have diminished so I threw back my bedding. The trouble with that was that there was then plenty of naked flesh to attract the mosquitoes, which were a menace. We had "mossie" nets and I tried one but that was even worse, I decided to rely on my anti-malaria tablets and take my chances. Perhaps because we were restless and wakeful we heard a leopard prowling around. The baboons heard it too and did not like it one little bit.

8

Return to the Farm

The next morning continued very hot and oppressive and I woke to find the bumps of several mosquito bites across my shoulders where the vicious little insects had filled their tanks with my blood. Pip had gone out for a last hunt while the rest of us fished unsuccessfully until mid-morning. We had just walked back to the camp when Pip came in with a kudu cow. The weather was so heavy that for the remainder of the day everyone lounged about reading and drinking gallons of lemon tea.

The hand pump had malfunctioned so that we had no amount of water in the camp, but the river was only a few yards away and as it was the same water when all was said and done, Pip and I went off for a late wash and shave in the Zambesi. When we had finished our ablutions we were lounging on the beach watching the river while Pip told me of some of his experiences in the Rhodesian army. When they were in the bush, one of the things they did to protect their camp from nighttime attacks was to set booby traps. Fishhooks would be heated and straightened, then hammered through a thin flat piece of wood. On end of a cord was attached to the wood and the other end to the pin of a hand grenade. These devices were placed around the perimeter of the night's camp. The enemy invariably went barefooted and a barbed fishhook could not be shaken off. When the victim leapt up and hopped about in pain his actions would set off the grenade. "It sounds barbaric." Commented Pip. "But they were out to kill us."

Just then a hippo decided to evacuate its bowels not far from us, out in the river. The beast surfaces and pokes its massive hind quarters skywards until, at the moment of excrement the short stubby tail revolves rapidly like a propeller. Muck spreaders had nothing on that! We laughed when I reflected that we washed in that water. Oh well, I <u>felt</u> clean and at least we boiled what we drank.

Later on someone unearthed a few cigars and when we took our usual seats along the cliff edge for sundowners those who wanted to, puffed the weed as well. Red-billed teal were flighting along the river as the sun sank and the frogs began their nightly serenade. Even after dark the temperature must have been over 80F. For all that we still made a large fire and sat down to a supper provided once more by Pip – kudu liver, onions, sudza and beans. A couple of bottles of wine to complement the meal and all was well with the world.

Pip and I tied the carcass of the kudu to the biltong racks in readiness for the hyenas. They came in quietly that night. So quietly that the first we knew of their presence was a crash and an irritated snarl as the scavenger realized that the carcass was tied down. There was only a moment's hesitation however, before we were treated to a terrific sound of cracking bones, for all the world like someone crunching brittle gingerbread biscuits. The chomping was intermixed with fiendish chuckles and laughter and then silence. Within half an hour that carcass, as big as a donkey, had completely gone. Every scrap cleared up. A few days later, back at the farm, when we were going over our mini-adventures I mentioned the hyenas. Nigel said. "Yes, I was a bit concerned when those blighters showed up. They always do of course, as soon as you've got meat in the camp, but they tend to get bolder and they are not averse to sneaking into camp and chopping anything that shows outside a sleeping bag – usually some poor so and so's face. For their size, they have the most powerful jaws of any animal and can inflict serious damage."

The hyenas had had a good meal on the night in question and thank goodness cleared off for pastures new. It was our last night in the Valley and the elements gave us a send off in the form of a violent thunderstorm. Great sheets of lightning flashed and flickered illuminating the mountains on the Zambian horizon in a most spectacular way. A few minutes of this and then we could hear the rain coming. It hit us and drove us into the open-ended shelter. Inside of an hour the storm had passed and it wasn't long in the sultry heat before our beds were dry enough for re-occupation.

The next morning *Sunday 25th October 1981* we struck camp and drove through the bush towards chirundu over tracks that were hardly affected by the rain. Had the rains come earlier we may have had to cut short our stay as the tracks become impassable. On our last stretch through the bush we saw wart hog, saddlebill stork, tawny eagle, bushbuck and the inevitable impala. The baobab trees were coming into flower, which reminded me that it was spring in Africa. Pip and Pam, only a few hundred yards behind us, glimpsed a herd of 300 buffalo. The bloody tsetse were biting to the last and were to give me cause for some amusement a little later. We had got out onto the main border road and just before we left the bushveldt had to pull off into a large sheet iron building. It was big enough to take at least three big lorries. Nigel explained. "Any vehicle leaving the fly belt has to be sprayed with disinfectant to kill any tsetse that is hitching a lift." What I expected upon entering I am not sure. Hoses and sprinklers I suppose, certainly not a lone African armed with a flit pump! Our trucks looked lost in that hanger like building. The man approached and gave us a single squirt into the cab; another into the back and that was it.

As the truck left the bush and began its bumpy climb up the escarpment I turned to look back over the Zambesi Valley with the knowledge that for as long as I live I am unlikely to set foot in a place more wild and natural. A place paradoxically full of danger and peace, thrills, magical noises, hot brooding silences and secret serene corners. Mentally I blessed my host for introducing me to this, his special place.

At Marongora we had to check out and in the process, met the young ranger again. During the coming wet season and he was off for a spell of leave. Pip and Pam said their goodbyes too for they were heading directly back to their farm at Centenary. We took the road to Makuti and then Karoi. Nigel asked if I would take over for a bit so I drove from Karoi to Sinoia via Banket. A hundred odd miles, no licence, no insurance, no – well, hardly any brakes and a forty-gallon barrel of petrol in the back. Luckily, there was little or no other traffic and certainly no police. We had a break at Sinoia so Corona showed me the famous caves. Then on again until we reached the great dyke – a range of hills rich in minerals including gold and chromium. At this point Nigel took over again so that I could look out for ostriches. We were lucky enough to see just one and a pair of oribi which for me, were another new antelope.

Stopped briefly at Salisbury to drop off the canoe and to collect Mike's son Guy, who wanted a lift to his boarding school near Marandellas. Guy rode in the back of the truck happily chewing on a strip of biltong presented to him by his grandfather. We left the boy at his school and made the last leg back to the farm by 6.30 pm where, after a bath and a gin and tonic, we were all ready to tumble into bed. The first bed with a roof over it for the past ten nights.

Monday 26ᵗʰ October 1981 We were up and about early for breakfast, after which I went with Nigel to dip some of the cattle. The last lot were going through when Richard drew up to invite me to see the tobacco being planted. In the truck were seedlings from the nursery near Richard's house. While we were driving along he told me that the seed is so fine it is first sown in water through a watering can and two grams plants a whole bed three feet wide and forty-five feet long. When they have grown enough to plant out the ideal seedling is six inches from root to small top leaf and about as thick as a pencil. The field had been ridged like oversized potato ridges and a spud wheel at the rear of the ridging plough equally spaced holes to receive the plants. Women took bags of seedlings and laid one against each hole. Slowly behind them crawled a tractor pulling a water bowser, from which sprouted five hoses. Five men watered the holes and in their wake five more men, with hand adzes, pulled open the hole, inserted a plant and heeled it in with the curved back of the adze. Thus, at a slow walking pace, the field was planted with tobacco, five rows at a time. While this is going on the previously planted seedlings are topped off with a few handfuls of topsoil. Finally, more girls spread powder to deter the first pests.

Later on the crop is sprayed twice against other pests and diseases, after which it is allowed to grow twenty leaves high, which takes it to about six feet. The top is then taken out to prevent flowering and to encourage filling out lower down the plant. If it is dry too early the plant will not germinate properly and will be short and thick, which is not good. Richard said that the half inch of rain we had yesterday helped in that with less manual watering to do the workers had planted more on this day than three or four days the previous week. We spent quite a while driving back and forth collecting more bags of seedlings from the nursery and ferrying them to the field and then off to check how work was progressing on the new house. The thatching was now going very well.

There were two little diversions as we made our way in the direction of lunch. We were approaching a kopje when jaws jumped out of the truck and tore off towards the pile of boulders yapping as only a terrier can. "He's after monkeys." Grinned Richard but his grin faded when we heard the challenging "Whaaoooff!" which identified the challenger as a baboon. "Oh hell, they're bad news." Said Richard. "They play havoc in tobacco." Half a mile farther on Richard stopped the truck and pointed to the track just in front of us. We got down for a closer look as a dung beetle rolled a two-inch diameter ball of cow dung across the road and up the far verge. The beetle was an inch long and lays its eggs in the dung. When the young hatch they live on the cacoon for the first day or so of life.

It rained again in the afternoon so later on Corona, Nigel and I drove to the new house, collecting Richard en route. The thatch was completed on one wing but after a somewhat forceful discussion, my hosts agreed that another doorway was in the wrong place and gave instructions for new one to be knocked through in a better position. Once again the total freedom of the country was brought home to me. To do that in the UK it would have taken a month or more to amend plans and bring in building inspectors and goodness knows who else. It was the same with the telephone line. Before my eyes men were erecting a line of beautifully straight gum poles in readiness for the installation of the cable. As an aside I will mention here that there were so few dwellings with a telephone that when any call was made the phone rang in every farmhouse in the locality. But, each number rang differently, for example the Thornycroft's number was Marandellas 34 so the instrument rang three, a seconds gap and then four times and it was remarkable that in a very short space of time even I recognised when the call was for "us" and subconsciously ignored all the rest.

Driving back to Richard's house we stopped to turn off the irrigation pump that was watering a field of maize and then dropped in for a pot of tea served by Gunstan, Richard's cook-boy. Later on Richard joined us for supper, which was a very palatable serving of roast kudu. The main course naturally inspired talk of past hunts in the Valley and of visits by kudu to the farm where Nigel always spared them.

Tuesday 27ᵗʰ October 1981 Early in the morning Richard's cook Gunstan had collapsed and died, it was thought from a heart attack. The police came down but gave the ok for a burial. Richard came to join us for breakfast and gave us all the details – such as there were. When I went with Richard on his rounds all the talk at the tobacco ridges was that Gunstan had been killed by witchcraft and that someone in the compound had put a curse on him! Richard commented grimly that in these cases the problems really start when someone is accused. It is usually a person who is not well liked who is picked out as the "witch."

Just driving around the farm roads we had a close encounter with six yellow-billed kites all catching and eating flying ants. This reminded Richard that the day before he had seen a huge king cobra, not the Indian variety. The reptile lived in a disused anthill. Further along the road we spotted three two-inch long spitting beetles.

The truck swung round to a standstill behind Nigel's house where I was surprised to see an aircraft hanger of sorts. It was a framework hanging with tattered and holed tarpaulins. Within was a light aircraft, a Piper Super Cub. A further surprise came when Richard invited me to see the farm from the air. Apparently, to take off, this little aeroplane needs just enough rough grass to be able to reach a speed of 80 mph. We bumped over some very rough grass and soon became airborne. At first it seemed as though the engine was rattling and roaring and the whole fuselage vibrating without us making much forward progress, but it was an illusion. The sun was getting low throwing objects and features on the ground into clear and sharp relief. We dived down towards the big dam, getting a ducks eye view of its destination. Banking round we did a couple of circuits of the farm and were able to see just what a large area it covered. As we landed I reflected that until I came to Africa I had never flown before.

Wednesday 28th October 1981 The previous day Nigel had tried out that new trout rod on the dam and the result of his efforts was our breakfast on this morning. Bream, which was quite delicious and left me wanting more. I had hardly wiped the crumbs from my mouth when we were on our way to dip cattle over at "*Sheffield.*" 213 year-old calves and 165 weaners were to be dipped. 14 of the yearlings were missing and so poor old Silvester, the cattle boy responsible for this herd, was told that he would forfeit his dollar bonus this week. Nigel said they had "baleekad" – ie strayed. Cows were called "Mombhi's and the calves, or in fact any infant, including human, were pickanins.

We drove around to see if we could locate the strays and found ourselves near imire and so called in on Johnny Travers. There was no sign of the beasts so we headed for lunch.

Late afternoon we were intending to go down to the dam near the new house but had to wait for the procession of Gunstan's funeral. A tractor and trailer came along the farm road carrying the body along with fifty or more singing Africans. There was a hold up when they discovered that the grave had not been dug wide enough. After a few minor adjustments with spades, the funeral went ahead.

At the new house we talked for a while and then Nigel and I took out the canoe. There are 170 acres of water and it was very beautiful as the sun sank. While it was light we saw purple, squacco and great white herons, egrets, reed cormorants, pied kingfisher and hundreds of swallows. Beaching the canoe, we re-joined Corona to kill off a bottle of vino to the sound of cassius roaring goodnight at imire, four miles away. Back at the house we finished the kudu with baked potato, beetroot and onion. In a quiet moment with Corona I felt the need to say that although I was not an excitable person and did not shout "Wow!" or "Yeeeha!" at every new incident it did not mean that I had not been thrilled or taken it all in, in my own way. I did not want my hosts to think I hadn't enjoyed my visit to the valley. Corona smiled and said. "Don't worry, you are of the same calm temperament as ourselves. Nigel is very choosy who he takes to the valley because we know its not everyones cup of tea. We guessed that you, with similar interests to us, would take to it and we weren't wrong."

Thursday 29th October 1981 On my last day I rose early, to walk perhaps five miles on the farm roads and vleis for a final look around. Josie the house girl asked if I would take photographs of her and the cook for their respective families. Naturally I obliged and sent the prints to them later on after processing. In readiness for his photograph Lovemore, the cook dived into his quarters and re-appeared fully changed into a sparklingly clean and freshly pressed white uniform. He looked very proud as he posed for the shot.

The morning was warm as I roamed through the long tawny grass by passing tall kopjes until I cut into a farm road again. By midday the atmosphere grew heavy and it came as no surprise when, after lunch a thunderstorm rolled up and rumbled around the neighbourhood. While the storm crashed and flickered outside I was packing for my return home. As Nigel and Corona drove me to Salisbury we saw twenty adbin storks and right at the last moment as we pulled into the airport a black korhaan flew past. What a good bird to end with. We shared a supper at the airport restaurant before we went our separate ways – my friends back to the farm and I onto a Heathrow bound jumbo jet with indelible memories of a fenman's African adventure.

9

A Letter from Africa

A selection of letters received after my visit when many town names were changed and Marondellas became Marondera

A duck shoot

22nd March 1982
Marandellas

Dear Phil

Many thanks for your double-barrelled airmail. Inevitably the second barrel arrived first but only by a couple of days and was nevertheless welcome for all that. Also your letter to Corona, your (*sketch of a*) fenman admiring prehistoric art gave several giggles. She thank goodness is now home again, though still on one crutch and likely to remain so for some weeks. Pretty agile nonetheless though the less accessible rock art is currently more in vogue.

Here I'm just coming to the end of one of the most hectic tobacco harvests I can remember. By Tuesday I shall be over the lump and with only half a dozen scattered barns left to reap and cure. But we've had an incredibly fast ripening season – largely owing to the drought – and for the past four weeks solid its been a case of reaping three barns a day with an increasingly weary looking labour gang – which means you have twenty in various stages of curing and conditioning. Three up, three down daily and its been quite a battle. We've lost quite a bit through over ripening, but have got 120 barns through with possibly a dozen only to come. Not a very high quality crop but at least its there. Brilliant bit of timing by Richard who dashed off to

101

Switzerland six weeks ago and has been sliding up and down alps ever since and due back on Saturday this week. However, in many ways I've enjoyed getting into the saddle again and it'll be up to him to sweep up the mess.

All this is gossip by the way. Tobacco crisis followed by Cattle crisis and its now some thirty hours later. I was going to give you a ball-by-ball commentary on one of the most fascinating mornings I have ever spent while I was still bubbling. I still am to some degree. Talk of fair weather fowling – A friend of mine some 20 – 30 miles North of here has built half a dozen or so biggish dams/weirs down his length of a tumbling river – dams half to one and a half miles in length in wooded msasa country all ups and downs and inlets. A very well off and efficient 3rd generation farmer whose hobby is ducks. He feeds his two outside dams pretty extravagantly throughout the year. Never shoots near them but studies crops etc where the birds are feeding and tries to intercept the flight lines. At the moment there are probably 5-600 knob nose drakes and 20 or 30 gyppy geese or spurwing. The knobbies were leaving the dams early and feeding on a neighbours groundnut lands who had an Af. with a tin can trying to act as a scarecrow.

Peter rang me Saturday night and said would I like to be there for a flight at 5.45 the next morning. The answer was in the affirmative. – strange. I don't know if you can picture a steepish valley with big msasa trees down most of one side, a high reed bed in the middle. Three guns straddling it and a fourth, way behind. The sun starting to lip the horizon behind us, the veldt grass brown and waving and the light just tipping the topmost leaves of the trees in front and creeping downwards as the sun rose. And above a sky of purest clear blue without a fleck of cloud.

A knobbie looks a clumsy great bird. Put him off the water and perhaps he is. Give him airspace and he definitely is not. These birds had been airborne for one or two miles. The first appeared just before 6.00 and from then till 7.45 there was never a dull moment. Over half were well out of shot. The others may or may not have been just in. I know I never fired at anything that wasn't vertically overhead, reckoning that ten degrees either side would be spraining my gun – and the odd few that put their face in the pattern were real tail-waggers. Not many did. I was right hand gun and must have fired thirty cartridges for the seven I collected – nor did I feel I was shooting badly. All fell in the patch of reeds 80 yards behind and below me and Misty never lost a bird. And finally the geese came. Three lots of gyppies and two of spurwing, but those we weren't shooting. It was the sheer and utter beauty that was so indescribable. That flawless blue sky and the sunlight reflected on the birds from below. Snow-white bellies and coaly wings clear etched against it. From my stand you could sometimes get a flicker through the branches ahead, but birds coming to me weren't clear till they were thirty degrees in front, though most were slanting across me. I had a superlative view of those going over the other guns. We all got quite enough shooting – but the tally only amounted to 14 birds, which in fact was quite enough. Those birds were high – possibly too high for two and a half inch sixes. But a sight for the gods. An un-African quarry in a setting utterly African and a picture to stay with you for a lifetime. Fowling? I suppose you could call it that – but with a difference.

I must away and look at my sorrowing cattle and my revolting tobacco. I weaned the first 53 calves this morning so the night will be full of lamentations!

Love to you all
Nigel

Gerry in the wars

Marondera
15-17th July 1983

My Dear Phil

A quite magnificent letter from you awaiting our return – and two days prior to our departure, a packet of disposable razors – a happy thought and quite immaculate timing. Lord, you do write remarkably interesting letters, and all about the sort of thing I, at least, want to hear about. I'm hastening to reply as the next few months may be a shade hectic and without much chance of putting pen to paper – and just at the moment there is a bit of a lull.

Bird wise, wasn't as exciting as last year, but we had great fun. The carmines hadn't arrived yet – only saw one trio circling way up. A few white fronted bee-eaters – plover, gyppy geese and the odd saddlebill stork and cormorants made up the river stuff. One goliath heron and fish eagles and to me, the plum of the whole lot was a pair of spoonbills that flew over towards dusk one evening. The outline of those beaks is unmistakable, however high. Inland I saw racquet tailed rollers and queleas – I have never seen the like – billion upon billion. At one time we had a cloud of these little birds passing up the river for nearly half an hour without a break – at one period tiger (*fish*) were jumping at them. On another occasion in the bush, Gerrit and I were about a mile from t'others and *we saw* a great cloud of dust rising above the treetops from where they were. Queleas rising – and this was the dust stirred up by their wings. Mike, who was with the other lot said it was one of the most incredible things he'd ever seen – acres of brown carpet taking off.

Gerry and I had a thriller of a morning; in fact saw a lion and lioness to start with. He with a fair, though rather ragged mane – she as sleek as a well fed pussy cat. And a couple of hours later, back in the real bush, the jammy bit. We ran into a herd of buffalo completely unexpectedly who hadn't a clue we were there and were feeding slowly, slowly towards us. Must have been 250 of them. We froze and slowly sat down, plumb in the open. We had their wind and they moved quite oblivious to us. The nearer rank, mostly cows with calves – bony old besoms they were too – was within 25 yards (measured later) and still coming when one caught a movement of my hand as I turned the camera for another shot – they wheeled like a flock of knot and the stampede fairly shook the ground and raised almost as much dust as the quelea had. But, what a sight to have seen – Gerry remarked drily. "I think they were quite close enough, especially with cows and calves in the lead." There were several bulls – we actually saw one mounting a cow – and we had quite an argument as to which we would have taken and just how we would have tried to get in to the one of our choice. The sad part came that evening when the back of the camera came off while changing the film and the whole roll was ruined. Cameras are NOT my strong point.

Apart from that big herd of buffalo we saw no real weight of game, but one or other of us came up with just about everything there was in the area – elephant, lion, rhino, buff, eland, kudu, waterbuck, zebra – down the line to the tiny grysbok. Some good views of bushbuck and impala everywhere. Each of us took out one impala and that's pretty well what we fed on – and if you can tell me of anything much nicer than fresh impala liver fried over a fire of mopane logs in the dusk, I'd like very much to try it. We also got a few guineas and francolin and one afternoon coming back late saw half a dozen little parties of sand grouse flipping through the tree tops for all the world like woodcock in the gloaming... but they, alas, were not on licence.

Evenings were fairly musical. Lions very talkative most nights. Hyenas there, but not wildly chatty and the terrific deep hippo chorus – a very lovely orchestra. One night we picked up a pair of honey badgers by torchlight, snuffling round our rubbish pit.

The fishing was fun, without any real highlight. Only one tiger reached double figures and not very many small ones.

Corona got some good Nkupi and chesser – the former up to 5 lbs and fun on light tackle. Vundu were the main excitement and we got five with the biggest at 72 lbs and the smallest 40 + and were broken a dozen times. I had one great battle and fought the creature a good quarter mile down the river before he tied me round a rock or tree stump 100 yards from the shore and we parted company. I was just about beat anyhow. Mike was the killer – as soon as he hooked one he'd leap into a canoe and follow it – actually rather a tame performance till it came to the gaffing! Getting a 70lb vundu into a small canoe in midstream is apt to be damping.

The tragedy came last Saturday. I was woken at 5.00 am by a voice calling "Nigel, Gerry has been badly bitten." Went over – he was sleeping 20 yards away – to find him still conscious with half his face torn away – slight exaggeration – cheek bone laid bare, one eye lid hanging across his nose, the bridge of which appeared to be missing and a bone deep cut clear across his forehead and more or less lying in a pool of blood, Very messy. Did what first aid we could – wash, disinfect, swab and bandaged lightly. Wrapped him up in blankets and into the back of a truck and off on the four hour hike to Kariba where we found a Dr and nurse who sedated him and generally tidied up before he was despatched by ambulance to Salisbury, 350 miles away.

Saw him yesterday – exactly one week later, here at Wedza, happy as a grig and his face looking no worse than if he'd had a couple of rounds with Joe Louis. The Salisbury quack had done a truly remarkable job of sewing him up – sixty-six stitches worth! - And when they're out and the swellings down a bit you'll hardly see any difference than before – and best of all, his eyeball is in place and sight as good as ever.

Of course, we all thought – hyena – so did the parks blokes at Marangora, but dawn told a different tale. Definite lion tracks through the camp and you could see where the perisher had turned off towards Gerry's bed – we photographed and drew scale drawings and finally convinced the parks wardens it <u>was</u> a lion. Certainly they'd been talking round the camp pretty close in the previous two nights – hyena too, of course. But, very un-lion like conduct – he'd made no effort to drag Gerry off so it obviously wasn't hunger. Personally I think he was just wandering through and didn't like the sound of Gerry's snoring so gave him a "shut up" tap. Gerry's own suggestion that he mistook the snores for the mating call of a lioness doesn't really hold water, as I doubt if G. would have got off so lightly!

But you may be sure that for the remaining three nights we slept with loaded guns alongside. Despite alarums and excursions it was a happy camp and a more than even bet that G. and I at least, will be down again next year.

Don't know when I'll get another chance to write. We're flying straight through on the way out, but dropping off in England for a week or so on our return – hopefully sometime early November. Will let you know when we have more idea – it would be grand to see you again, though I take your tale of the "owed meal" with a slight pinch of salt!

Love to you all
Nigel

Gerrit von Memerty keeps an eye on a Bull Elephant

Nigel's last zambesi camp

Marondera
11th October 1987

My Dear Phil
    I'm going to start a letter anyway – though heaven knows when I'll finish. Affairs a shade cramped at the moment – house seems eternally full. But I've been casting envious eyes at the moon and wondering if an early wigeon or goose has found its way into your line of fire as yet…

…All out of the blue Gerry von Memerty - who has taught me most of what I know of big game – drew me quietly aside and murmured in my ear. "I'm off down the valley day after tomorrow – it'll be an all male camp. What about it?" I am far too decrepit to hunt these days and said so – but the thought of being among all the noises of the night and the big river sounded like a glimpse of heaven – so there was only one possible answer and at 5.30 in the morning he appeared, dumped my bedding roll into his Land Rover and away. We were in that **A** camp area at the foot of the gorge, where you launched the canoe.

He then goes on to describe the events of the camp, which are now familiar to the reader so we will skip to the end of the letter.

    Then the final day – a nephew of Gerry's had come up from Chirundu by boat – a little 12 foot fibre glass affair with an outboard – the previous night and proposed tackling the gorge the next day. T'others were out after their second buffalo, they'd got the first earlier and it was all cut up and hanging as biltong – would I like? I would, as I'd never been up the gorge before – always too busy hunting! It was tremendously worthwhile. The gorge is about 17 miles long, towering precipitous hills maybe 2000 feet either side and in many places barely forty-five degrees of sky. Turbulent swirling waters as the river is compressed to maybe only 50 yards width – heaven knows how deep – great whirlpools ten feet across. Some of the carvings wrought in the rock faces by the currents of centuries beggared any form of modern sculpture – and I had no camera. Vast, and at times truly awe–inspiring. We got up to some 200 yards of the Kariba dam wall – then turned to drift down using the motor purely to keep out of trouble. Mike and Hamish were drifting a small live bream in case of emergencies. I wasn't fishing. An 11 lb tiger hit Hamish – and in that water the ensuing ten minutes were full of action.

We were drifting away fairly fast when it happened. Must have crossed a shallower underwater ridge when crash – the boat tipped just about vertical – all loose stuff flipped straight overboard and we clutched what we could to avoid following suit as she slowly came down on her keel again. My first thought was we'd crashed a rock. But not so. A Bloody great hippo – who had no business to be in that kind of water – had taken a dim view of the boat and charged from below. Cracked the hull right along the keel and four great tooth marks but miraculously not taking much water and entirely navigable. But we were lucky. If it had overturned completely or if we hadn't managed to cling on, I doubt if we would have had a hope in that current. But – as I said – fun – in retrospect!

I'm now sitting at my desk chewing a bit of buffalo biltong with a wild Egyptian goose picking up maize on the lawn not 15 yards away. Life has its moments. Sun going down and egrets and cormorants starting to fly in to roost in the reed beds across the dam.

     My love to you all
     Nigel

Nigel's last letter

Marondera
22nd August 1988

My Dear Phil
This probably won't be a very exciting letter but may
serve to keep in touch as likely you won't hear from me for a
couple of months or so and I shan't be going down to the valley
next month either. But I shall be thinking of you and the
Washes in September with a certain amount of envy, listening
for the sibilance of wings in the half-light. I still remember with
some joy that pre-season mock flight I did with you when we
reckoned IF we had shot straight we might between us have
collected four duck. And the black silhouettes of plover and the
fairy glimpse of a snipe into that rather furrowed bit of flooded
grass – and the almost degrading comparison of having a
thousand hand reared mallard pushed over my head a fortnight
later on the edge of wales –
Anyway, Corona is off to Australia on Thursday for six weeks
or so to attend a world conference on rock art – bushman's
paintings to you and me: HQ Darwin where some 300
professors and such are congregating. She has to read a paper
on the subject in this country. Quite an accomplishment and I'm
rather proud and I must say the acres of drawings and tracings
she has made up are pretty astounding and beautifully done.
I'm off meanwhile down to Natal for a fortnight to stay with
one of the young – Hugh – I don't think you met him – all
among the racehorses and a possible trout. Back home for a few
days and then probably flip over to England mid-September for
a couple of weeks. I sadly fear little chance of getting across to
your part of the country, much as I'd like to, as I'm becoming
deplorably egg bound these days and can hardly walk a yard
and no transport. I am more likely to find my way across the
Zambesi valley than any modern town or station!
But if there's a chance I will, as I'd love to see you both again
and possibly sink a pint – Maybe I shall find a confiding pigeon

110

to come down to a decoy, but otherwise see little chance of losing off a gun, though will probably taste a grouse or a partridge again....

The letter goes on for three more pages with news from the farm and it was not possible to foresee that within three weeks of writing it my dear old friend would be dead. I planned to drive over to Shropshire to visit him at his brothers and when the time came I telephoned Guy to see if he had arrived. I felt as if I had been punched in the solar plexus when Guy said. "I am sorry. Nigel died last week. You are on the list of people I have to tell."

He had got to his son's in Natal but while there his emphysema caught up with him and he died in Pieter Maritzberg hospital with three of his sons at his side. Poor Corona received the news in Australia. Over the next days and weeks I received from various people several copies of the tribute printed below.

A Tribute to the Memory of Nigel Thornycroft
By David Hamilton Memorial Service, Wedza St. Cross,
evening Thursday 15th September 1988

To try to do justice to the memory of Nigel in a matter of five minutes or so is of course quite impossible. To recall a life of adventure, of exploits of the bizarre nature, of qualities and intricacies of character – all this and so much more, ought really to be recorded in a book and I do feel that the family should consider this at some later stage. The volume would never have a dull moment; dramatic, instructive – Nigel had a fund of knowledge, particularly upon things natural – and at times uproariously funny.

Nigel was always inclined to take both himself and the situations he found himself in, extremely seriously. But often when he looked at them in retrospect, that glorious chuckle of merriment would take over. In fact I well remember one occasion, which I think, was probably the last game of cricket he ever played in. The match was played at Shrewsbury against the Gentlemen of Shropshire, a very correct and dignified team. Nigel came out to bat late on a lovely English summers evening. His hair was bright yellow, so much so that he rather resembled a punk rocker. His arms were daubed with purple blotches, as no doubt were his legs beneath his flannels. He had a decidedly bad limp as he went out to the wicket and he was quite oblivious as to the sensation he caused. In fact, he had been dipping cattle two days previously on Merryhill. He'd somehow got dosing mouti all over his hair, he'd plastered gentian violet all over the cuts and bruises he invariably got whenever he worked on the farm and a cow had kicked him on the shin.

There are so many aspects of life that one associates Nigel with, but first and foremost comes Corona. Nigel and Corona were as one, and I'm quite sure that all of us are thinking of her at this moment, just as she is most probably thinking of us and the family here in Wedza.

But apart from Corona and his beloved family, one visualises all the other loves of his life. Wildfowling in England, chasing guinea fowl and calling his gun dog all the names under the sun as it hares off after a buck. Hunting in the valley – what other man has killed a buffalo with No.6 bird shot? Fishing up to his armpits in water casting for a trout, or stalking up from gulley with arms outspread as the bowler lets go the ball at the batsman.

All these memories and so very many more. But they were all, really just the trappings of his life. Creativity was his real goal – creativity in harmony with nature.

Merryhill is really the perfect example of what he expected and indeed achieved in the form of creation, and often achieved at the expense of any financial gain. But with Nigel, money, motorcars and machinery came very low on his list of priorities.

Of course he loved people, he was an exceptionally good listener and conversationalist and he loved children, particularly when he could introduce them to the magic of the natural world, as his grandchildren have often experienced.

He also loved solitude and at times this proved to be rather disconcerting. On one occasion Pat and I were fishing on a very lonely stretch of the Gaerezi River and were totally unaware that anyone else was on the river at all. Nigel appeared around a bend, with his poacher's jacket, rod and net. He took one look at Pat, who was up to her waist in water and with obvious disgust turned away and carried on half a mile upstream. He got to Black Duck pool where he came across me. He literally exploded. "Perish the thought David! The ruddy place is like Brighton Beach on a Bank Holiday." With that he stalked off further upstream and that was the last we saw of him.

One might really term Nigel an eccentric; there are so many adjectives by which one can describe him. Loving and considerate, and at times positively infuriating. Tolerant and caring and at times as stubborn as a mule. Generous and gentle or as dogmatic as anyone could be. These were but a few of the characteristics that made up the man. But above all, he was a person of such high principles, which he lived up to with the utmost dignity, few of us could ever hope to measure up to them in any way.

"He nothing common did – or mean – upon that memorable scene." And in Nigel's case, that memorable scene was his whole life span.

From Corona –
Tragedy in the bush

Marondera
10th June 1990

My Dear Phil

We are just back from **B** camp, all the boys and wives except Pip and Pam who couldn't make it. The first day Mike and Richard went off early hunting. The hunters are usually back for a late lunch, and when 2.00 o'clock and then 3.00 o'clock went I was beginning to get worried – perhaps wounded a buffalo and were following it up – or what? It was nearly dark when they returned. What had happened was they had shot an impala and had a chase after it. When they tried to find the jeep it wasn't there and it was only after walking about 5 Ks each way along the roadway that they realised it wasn't the right road. They must have walked over the right road and come upon another one. By the time they got back to the first road the boy with the jeep had driven it off expecting to meet them. It might have had really serious effects, as it was Mike was totally dehydrated, as they had had no water. Richard stood up better, possibly because he doesn't smoke and Mike does. Anyway alls well that ends well, but it must have been nasty for them.

The second night Richard was trying to put together a small gas bomb but a candle was close by and the whole thing exploded. Luckily he was not burned and managed to stamp out the blaze.

Then Mike unfortunately wounded a buff. Very sad as it was "his" camp. They tracked it for hours but never did get up to it. Then the really shocking tragedy happened. Gerrit von Memerty, (I'm sure you will remember him from **C** Camp?) got <u>killed by an elephant</u>. He and Hermanus, a great friend of his had gone after a buffalo. They had a long fruitless walk and were coming back to the jeep, walking in very thick jesse when they saw a baby elephant – they had barely registered the fact when they realised that they had walked into a herd of females

114

and young. They all scattered in different directions (the tracker was with them) and the last Hermanus saw of Gerrit was that he was being chased by two elephants. After he had managed to shake off the one pursuing him and the herd had moved off he tried to find Gerrit and only made contact with the tracker by firing shots to alert him to where he was in the bush. They searched for an hour but as it was getting dark had to give up and come back to camp.

Of course we hoped against hope that Gerrit had been knocked out only and would be found in the morning. The men all went off early contacted the ranger and his tracker and they found Gerrit – dead. It must have been very quick – it would seem that the two elephants chasing him had stopped before reaching him but that a third had come straight in and run him through in two places. Fortunately for everyone concerned Mike Murray, Gerrit's wife's son was at the fishing camp close by and took over the job of breaking the bad news.

Poor Hermanus was distraught thinking there might have been something he could have done to save Gerrit, but in crises like this it all happens so quickly – and if you are being chased by an elephant you don't think of anyone else. Oddly enough after the first grief at losing a very dear friend it all seemed "right." He had loved the bush and all its animals and lived for them all his life – and he always said. "One of the bastards will get me in the end." It was how he would have wished to go, no doubt about that, but he was only 62 so it was too soon. We thought of packing up the camp but decided that was the last thing Gerrit would have wished so we stayed on and the whole atmosphere was happy – odd – but it was as if he was still with us all the time. I am sure he has met up with Nigel and is yarning of hunts past...

Much Love
      Corona

APPENDIX

Selected extracts from Corona's Game Books

I have mentioned earlier that I enjoyed reading the entries in my friends Game Books. Corona's in particular for its delightful little and sometimes not so little, pen and ink sketches of the fish, fowl or scenes recorded in its pages.

They are too good not to be shared and although they record Norfolk days in the 1920's and 30's long before she went to Africa they are part of the story and are not out of place here. In any case I think that most readers of this book will enjoy them as much as I have.

The very first entry is for the whole year of 1925, when Corona was 14 years old and had been given a .410 gun by her father. That season her bag was 2 rabbits, 14 waterhen, 2 duck and 6 rats. The next seasons bag included her first snipe and pheasant.

1928 saw much more activity with five days with the Eastern Counties Otter Hounds during August, including one where they killed a 20lb lady otter at Didlington. September brought with it the first invitations to shoots on neighbours farms - for example, 10th at Marham when seven guns shot 39 partridges, 2 snipe, 1 pigeon, 8 hares, 15 rabbit and a dove. Also fishing when the entry for 6th rather tetchily comments: *Narborough - somebody fishing in _my_ piece of water caught 2 pike and a trout weighing about a pound and a quarter - both pike were big fish.*

Beagling at Setch and goose shooting at Wells in October followed by pheasant days at Narborough Hall and Mr Hotblack's shoot, then riding her horse "Mike" with the West Norfolk Hunt made for a broadening of sporting experience for the young sportswoman. She managed to put her first woodcock in the bag - with the .410 on 8th January 1929 and ended the season with an entry, which reads: *February 24th - Self - from nursery window - I hooded crow.*

Spring 1929 was spent fishing at spots with intriguing sounding names such as - *Just above the swingy plank - Village bit - opposite policeman's house - under alder bush -and, above the railway bridge.* But 18th & 20th May records that JH and CEG (Corona) took creels of 11 trout averaging one and a half pounds each on Mayfly from beat 12 of the River Avon.

7th August of that year the otter hounds met at Hillington: *Drew down to the mill with touches of very stale drag. Left off at Babingley Bridge at 2.00 (Lunch 12.30)*

Never one to pass up a chance of a bit of sport the entry for 31st August 1929 seems to indicate that our heroine slipped away from a more social engagement: *Cockley Cley (Tennis Party, ahem!) - Wickham Fancy - 3 rainbow trout, 2 brown trout, 1 roach.* The bag of 64 partridges to six guns taken on 7th September at Chalk Farm gives some impression of the numbers of the grey partridge that were the norm in those days.

Pasted into the book at the start of 1930 is an extract from a French newspaper, which describes King George V salmon fishing. The translation runs thus:

He is an angler of the first force this King of Britain, behold him there, as he sits motionless under his umbrella patiently regarding his many coloured floats. How obstinately he contends with the elements. It is a summer day of Britain. That is to say, a day of sleet and fog and tempest but what would you, it is as they love it, those who follow the sport.

Presently the King's float begins to descend. My God, but how he strikes; the hook is implanted in the very bowels of the salmon. The King rises. He spurns aside his footstool. He strides strongly and swiftly towards the rear. In due course the salmon comes to approach himself to the bank. Aha! The King has cast aside his rod; he hurls himself flat on the ground on his victim. They splash and struggle in the icy water. But it is a braw laddie, the gillie, a kind of outdoor domestic, administers the coup de grace with his pistol. The King cries with a shrill voice "Hip Hip Hurrah!" On these red-letter days his Majesty

118

George dines on haggis and whisky grog. Like a true Scotsman he wears only a kilt."

I thought that might amuse salmon purists and it could be interesting to be in earshot of the comments of a highland gillie on hearing himself described as an outdoor domestic!

The Game Book entries for the spring of 1930 record the return, from Kenya, of Somerville Gurney, Corona's brother and it looks a though the siblings spent most of April and May at their fishing. On 22nd April Corona used a cast-net to catch 5 dace and 7 roach and 16th May at Hillington she and Somerville took 8 trout on a red spinner.

Late August and early September were spent at with other friends at Glensheil engaged in fishing, rough shooting and stalking. A note in the book tells the story of her friend Jane's (*Birkbeck's*) first stag. - *Mr Campbell, Colin, Johnnie and self went up the pony path towards the saddle as far as the ridge. Left ponies and climbed up. Saw a large party of stags and hinds on the skyline from Armisdale way. Waited half an hour. Colin, Jane and I went on, getting into a seven-pointer in forty minutes under the top of the saddle. - A good stalking day, very clear blue sky the whole time.*

Right across the top of the two pages of the book listing the sport in Scotland is a nice little sketch of a stalking scene and below, another showing Corona and Jane fishing from a boat on loch Duich when the catch was 16lbs of cod, whiting, saythe, gurnet and haddock.

Corona and one P Heywood for five morning flights visited Terrington Marsh between 3rd and 12th February 1931. They met with success on the 10th - *Terrington Windmill end. All clouds and strong wind off the land. Finished by raining hard. Moon last quarter - low tide. 4 geese (pinkfeet) 1 right & left.*

The famous Frank Cringle, professional wildfowler of Wells, was employed on 2nd February 1932 to act as guide to Mr

Murton, O. Rose, Corona and also Mr Smith and Mr Hancock. They were up at 4.30 am and taken across the channel near the lifeboat station and out on the sands of the East Hills. The note says that the wind was 100 mph and very cold. The geese went over too high and the total bag was a mallard and a golden plover.

As a present for Corona's 21st birthday a C. Cambell Coquhoun gave her a landing net. There is a very nice pencil sketch of the net, the frame of which appears to be made of wood, and a trout around a poem written by the donor. It reads:

"You see that beauty 'cross the stream
it is a trout, no dace or bream.
He's seen you - he is off his feed
For there's his wave - he's in that weed.
Just wade right in and I do bet
you'll get him in this landing net.

If you were wishing one to wed,
It might be Jack or cheery Ned
Then angle well and cast your fly
Without a plop, most gingerly:
and then with caution you will get
him safely in your landing net.

A carrier for all and sundry
All through the week, including Sunday;
You'll find it useful and I trust
Within its folds, you'll often thrust
The biggest trout that ere was met
Within this Camwam landing net.

Dawn flights at Fosdyke on the Welland estuary and near the Ouse estuary on a farm at Wootton featured during January and February 1933. One of Corona's companions on these wintry adventures was John Stephenson who was also a friend of

Douglas Bader. This was followed on 16th November of the same year by a morning flight at Terrington Marsh with Christopher Dalgety author of the sort after book *Wildfowling*. Corona nearly walked into a party of geese that had been dropped by the tide onto the mud close to the salt marsh. After a blank flight she was taken to inspect Dalgety's gunning punt.

A couple of weeks later Corona was to have gone punt gunning with Peter Scott, Christopher Dalgety and Mervyn Ingram but gale winds prevented that. However, after meeting at Scott's East Lighthouse home on the Nene estuary the four of them went to Holbeach to wait for geese coming in to Will Tinsley's farm. The geese did not come and the bag was a single mallard.

Corona got her chance to go out into the Wash punt gunning with Peter Scott on 2nd Jan 1934. They were out 12 hours, but did not get an opportunity for a shot. They did board a shrimp trawler for a break. For readers who are unacquainted with punt gunning I should point out that when stalking a company of duck the gunner and the stalker lie full length on their stomachs in the bottom of the punt. A note at the end of the entry reads - *"Felt a little shy of my posterior view when lying in the stalking position."*

It was all girls together during mid-May 1934 when Ruth Barclay and Patience and Jane Birkbeck joined Corona for a fishing holiday in Scotland. They took 40 trout from the burn at Kinloch Hourn and on the last day - 6 whiting and 3 flounders from the sea.

12th June 1934 is notable in that for the first time a certain N. Thornycroft appears in the book, fishing on Narford Lake with Corona and F Trowbridge.

The entries from 28th June until 10th July 1934 record the catches made when Salmon fishing in the locality of the River Vefsen in Norway. The party took a total of 100 Salmon weighing 1518 lbs + 4 Grisle (19lbs) an average weight of 15lbs. The largest fish went to 29lb and there were 12 scaling more than 20lbs. Corona took 16 fish totalling 239 lbs - the heaviest going to 28lbs.

Nigel Thornycroft appears again at the end of August and September, when Corona has obviously been invited to see the foxes at his fur farm at Blackborough End. They shot together on Nigel's land and on the coast. One evening flight at Terrington Marsh a Ruff was shot by Nigel. I believe this incident came to be included in his book *Fowler's Moon*. At Blackborough on 18th September Corona joined Nigel and his brothers - Gray and Guy for a day at the partridges. The bag was 14 brace plus 2 snipe, a hare and a rabbit. There are also sketches of Corona's new acquisitions for 1934 - a three inch chambered 12bore by Jeffery and a pair of Jodphurs! She went for morning flights at Terrington on 11th and 17th where she notes that there was a very good curlew flight but couldn't hit a haystack.

25th October 1934 Corona was in a shooting party at Barton Bendish when six guns made a bag of 40 brace of partridges, 7 pheasants and 8 hares. On 14th November she did a solo morning flight on Scolt Head and shot a snipe. Four days later the scene was the Wash coast at Fosdyke where she went with Peter Scott and Lady Hilton Young (*Scott's mother - watching*) for a morning flight. The note says that they crept out to the muds, to the left of the roosting geese and a skein headed for them as it grew light. Another gunner further down fired at some more geese but his shot made "their" birds rise and fly over too high. They saw about 1200 come in.

A day of mixed fortunes was how 20th December 1934 turned out. Corona was punt gunning with Peter Scott. Her note reads: *Towed the punt down with the motorboat to nearly end of the Nene main channel. Round another seven miles to wildfowling ground. Saw 34 scoters, several mergansers, 9 scaup, G.*

Crested Grebe, not many mallard and a lot of wigeon, which were very restless. Took the most right handed bunch in Glass eye a small lot but well bunched and got 10 of them. The only shot we could get. 10 wigeon...for one half tooth!

When she fired her face had been a little too near the big gun and enough to get a nasty smack in the face. An accompanying sketch shows a concerned looking Scott and Corona holding her mouth.

2nd and 11th January 1935 saw visits to Welney Wash by Nigel and Corona. On the first occasion just 1 snipe found its way into the bag. On the 11th they were accompanied by Michael Watson and the bag increased - although it all fell to Nigel's gun: 1 snipe, 5 shoveler and 2 teal. The next day the trio tried a dawn flight at Holbeach Marsh and collected 2 geese, a curlew and 2 golden plover. The note reads: *N. walked into the geese going out. Later a couple flew over having already been shot at by Donaldson. An almighty good shot.* Donaldson appears to have been a local wildfowler.

By 15th February it was back to Welney under a nearly full moon with a high wind. Just the two of them shooting. They had a good flight picking up 7 wigeon a pintail, a teal and a mallard.

The gales were still blowing from 20th February to 26th during which time the couple, with various friends accounted for 209 woodpigeons coming to the roosting woods. The best day was the 21st when the party included Nigel's father - Colonel Thornycroft and Harry Mullenger, Nigel's handyman and general factotum at the fur farm. Eight guns killed 110 pigeon.

At the fox farm there was a sandpit in the form of a gully, which abounded with rabbits. Nigel and Corona would sit at one side with .22 rifle and pistol and wait for the bunnies to come out. On the evening of 29th April 1935 they potted 8.

Run rabbit run - the sand pit at the Fox Farm at Blackborough End

From 14th June to 30th October 1935 Corona was in Finland and the stay there included quite a bit of fields sports. The story of that would almost make a book in itself so I will confine it to an entry headed ALGJAKT (which, if my scant knowledge of Scandinavian language serves me well translates to ELK HUNT.) HONGOLA October 20th, 21st, 24th 25th

By Saturday the whole party had collected for the big shoot. It was all taken very seriously and well just had beer to drink for dinner and were sent to bed early. Everyone previously had to go through a sort of test, shooting from 120 metres at a life size dummy elk on a pulley. First still, then moving up across a gap between two trees. - Good fun and good practice.

We were up by 6.00 on the 20th, everyone showing signs of strain and several owned to a sleepless night. The idea is to drive the elk with beaters, downwind to a line of guns. As we were armed with every weapon from a Colt revolver to the latest big game rifle it looked highly dangerous. Most of us had German or Finnish military rifles and there was one ancient bear gun.

The first drive was blank though speaking personally, every bird flying; every sound made my heart thump like a drum. The second drive Robbie heard something definitely coming to him put up his rifle and then found he was covering Eddie who had thought his place was bad or something. Just at that moment 3

124

bulls walked out near Gunor. He took careful aim - missed - had two more shots and the three elk went quickly on their way right past the spot where Eddie should have been. (He'd evidently never read A Father's Advice.) The rest of the day was blank and we got in at 5.00 pm very wet and cold.

Over the next couple of days, which were desperately cold and wet the party dwindled until the last two had to leave for a wedding. When they came back on the 23rd it was decided to go out again the next morning.

The guns this time weren't quite so aristocratic. Besides myself and Robbie were the chauffeur, the forester, the farm inspector, the cow manager and twenty beaters. The weather had changed to a hard frost - minus 4c at 6.30 am and when the sun came up it was glorious.

First drive - blank again. At the second we walked miles and miles to quite a new ground. I had a funny feeling that something might happen; there was a white horse at one farm yard and later, as we were getting into our places I got to a spot where I felt I must be and without my saying anything Robbie said. "Would you like to stay here?"

A forest fence ran across the front and ahead was thick green forest rising up on the right over a steep little hill. The only clear space was a little swampy clearing on the left. I settled down and after only five minutes of waiting they were coming at last.

First a confused mass of legs coming down the slope and small shafts of light dappling great dark beasts. They were making straight for the clearing on my left. I put up my rifle in readiness and from behind a big spruce trotted out first a cow - No. Little 'un - No. Now there must be a bull - and there he was, just one agonizing moment when I couldn't see the sights of my rifle against his dark hide - then crash! - and he was down. Heavens - what an awful moment - no sound from Robbie - perhaps it wasn't the thing to do, to break the middle of a drive? Ventured a feeble "Robbie?" and was furious to find my voice gone quite thin and trembly.

After that everyone came running up and the beaters went quite mad with excitement, giving me three cheers. It was all most embarrassing. He was only a young bull - four with two points but looked big enough. The rest of the day was blank and the following day too. The sequel to this is that George Ramsey and the forester went out at Palikais this last day - no dogs or beaters and in half an hour they ran into two bulls and shot one!

Rage and fury at Hongola.

By November our heroine was back home in Norfolk enjoying plenty of shooting. On 23rd She was at Runcton with Uncle Wal, Dan, Nigel and Mr English. The party shared a bag of 27 partridge, 39 pheasants, 6 hares, 1 woodcock, 1 pigeon and a waterhen, which was caught by Bill, Nigel's spaniel.

Two days later Corona was accompanied by Jack Coverdale and an obviously later note indicates that Coverdale served in the RAF during the war, was shot down over Germany and left her his shotgun.

18th December five guns, including Nigel Thornycroft were pigeon shooting at Westacre. After shooting 201 they packed up and three of them - Nigel, Stephen Johnson and John Birkbeck subsequently walked the water meadows below Colchester House. This little foray yielded - 5 teal, 4 snipe, 1 partridge, 6 rabbits, 2 pigeon and a sparrowhawk.

After the new year Corona had a programme of sport all worked out around the weekend beginning Friday 10th January 1936. However, things became complicated as the following entry describes:

10th Drove to Cromer for lunch. - Tommy Barclay, Peter Barclay and myself - shot 13 pigeons and a partridge at Trimingham.

11th Went to the meet at Elmham. (North Norfolk Hunt)

1.30 got home. Rang up Blackborough. Mrs G. said that Nigel had shot a goose the previous night, that there was a big lot in and he was going again that evening. Sickening news - last

126

night of the last full moon and having to go to the hunt ball that evening. N. was shooting at Walton so got in the car and went to find them. During the last two drives John B and I decided that we must flight and do the dance too. If we got a goose N was to come too!

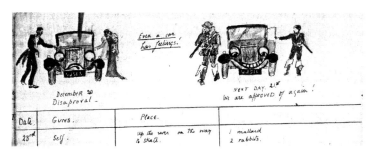

Date	Guns.	Place.	
23rd	Self.	Up the river on the way to Stake.	1 mallard 2 rabbits.

Even a car has feelings!

4.30 packed one suitcase for Ruth to take on from the dance and another with an evening dress in it while I got into marsh clothes.
5.30 At Blackborough. Robert Elwes there. N rushed in at 5.45 having stopped at Westacre for pigeons.
6.30 Terrington. (Marsh) Found an unpaddlocked gate and a sort of concrete "Regents Street"! That saved a lot of time so we waited in the car for the moon, due to show at 7.00. It didn't of course - there was barely a star showing. Went out at about 7.10 and spread out. Robert on the right, John, then Nigel on the left. The tide was coming in and one had to keep retreating back.

After some time the geese began to sound a bit. Robert's gun boomed out and shortly afterwards I heard a shout - had he got one? After listening for a bit - more shouts, which sounded panicky. I got in a bit of a panic myself and started off in R's direction. It was still very dark as the moon was clouded over - however I soon saw a figure, which turned out to be R. - completely lost! That put him right.

On getting back to my place a shot came from the other two. It was Nigel with a goose down, though I didn't know that then. The geese had begun to move at Roberts shot, a lot went over the other coast, but some were flying in to the fields behind us. I began to go back to the sea wall. It was then about 10.00 pm so the chances of ever getting back to the party seemed small. Then someone called from the angle of the sea wall which sounded as though N and J had gone back before me. After a little walking a figure came into view (The moon was showing by this time). I said. "John?" but it didn't answer so I sat down in the long grass and the one figure became two, which stood motionless - listening - and in a little while moved on towards the sea.

I continued my way to the wall and waited. Quite soon I heard N and J splashing along the edge of the tide and talking and they gave a shout for me. I did my best with a holloa, but nearly twenty minutes passed without them coming. I got rather furious because it was going to be awfully rude about the dance anyhow - it ended at midnight. Then there was a concerted view holloa from miles away to the right - they evidently thought I was asleep or lost - I went raging to the car, turned on the lights and hooted.

Well, it was 11.15 before we got the car started. They'd gone along the coast and met the other two who said they'd seen a <u>ghost</u> (me.) Then when they shouted for me they got a good piece of language from the strangers.

11.30 back at N's house.

12.05 At the abbey, Westacre in evening clothes + goose. The goose was subsequently pinched. History doesn't relate who by, a pretty shrewd suspicion.

There is a lovely sketch with the entry for 27th January 1936 which shows Corona about eighteen feet up a pine tree poking off a dead pigeon that had lodged in the branches. The caption reads - *"Why waste shells?"*

Earlier that day Nigel, his brother Gray Thornycroft, Susan Bonsey and Corona had shot at Holbeach, bagging a mallard, a hare, a pheasant, a curlew and a redshank. The note reads:

Caught by an old buster on Caldwell's marsh. Had no idea it was private. The sad part was that a lovely bunch of goldies (Golden Plover) *came right over just as the old man had left and of course, daren't shoot then.*

They were lucky to have been merely warned off as it was around this time that farmer Caldwell and his neighbours were suffering the predations of one Mackenzie Thorpe the well-known local poacher!

6th February 1936 records an evening at Terrington Marsh with Nigel. She writes: *Had found where the wigeon had been feeding - hoped it would thaw, but it was beginning to freeze as we got down. Went further out beyond the windmill - N got one, then we wandered back - and the wigeon had come in. Too sickening - we waited for them to come back again. N got three more. I think I should have had two - too slow my girl!*

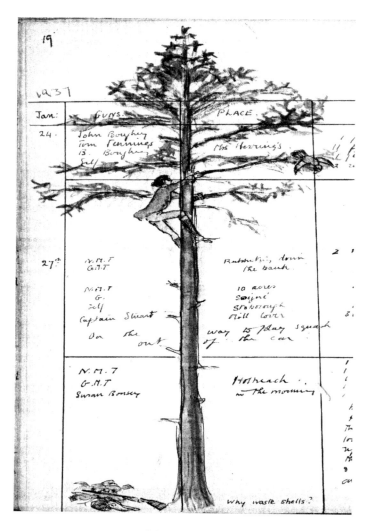

Why waste shells?

Pasted into the Game book is a letter from Nigel who had been itching to go punt-gunning with Peter Scott. It is dated 3rd March 1937.

My Dear Corona

Yes, it's happened at last. I went out with Peter last Friday and had just about the time of my life. I rang him up Thursday morning just on the off chance, but he was away. Thursday evening I had a bloke feeding here and in the middle of dinner the phone went. "Peter speaking; I've just arrived, if you've nothing better on tomorrow would you like to come out in the boat?"

The bloke with me must have thought I'd gone crazy, as I pushed him straight out of the house and went straight to bed. Not that I slept much, I was waiting for that alarm to go off. It was a lovely sunrise but a very dirty one. The whole sky lit up then faded away inside ten minutes. On the way to Sutton Bridge I spotted a pair of carrions by the roadside; dealt faithfully with one of them and thought it was a good omen. It didn't seem so good when I got there as it was blowing hard and Peter wasn't a bit sanguine even of going out. Moreover it was a blue sky and sunny and there had been gale warnings on the wireless overnight. However, by 8.30 we were afloat. P asked if I minded rowing a bit and rashly I said of course not.

Going out was a gift, we sailed straight out for about 3 or 4 miles and then we had to row, which wasn't so funny in that sea. But the birds... we saw three red necked grebes, several slavonian and black-necked and one great crested; a pair of great northern divers and several red-throated. Quite a few mergansers. Cormorants and shags everywhere. One black-necked grebe gave us some fun. The sandbanks were beginning to show and we got him between us and a sandbank about 50 yards off. For half a mile we kept him so, rowing like mad and he kept popping up very nearly alongside. Eventually he got tired of playing, dived and came up behind us. By now the rain was coming down in sheets and had been for the past hour. Glasses were fogged and visibility reduced to 300 yards. We hung about outside the sled for a bit (Scotsman's sled is a channel between sandbanks) but saw nothing, so we rowed on. Then something black appeared, lining the waters edge. Wigeon? We moved on cautiously and discovered a fine mussel scaup.

131

The banks were well out of the water and we were in a channel perhaps a quarter mile across. It was a very low tide, as P. had never seen that particular scaup before. It did look like wigeon too. While were still examining it, a bunch of about a hundred wigeon came flying low over the bank and pitched in our channel, a quarter mile away; followed by another and another; five bunches in all. I was feeling quite weak. One lot of about 200 went ashore on the far side and we pushed over, but though they were bunched beautifully there were ten outliers. As a forlorn hope P. decided to try to move them into the main body, so we lay down and he pushed. Some 200 yards from them he stopped. Another bunch had gone ashore on the opposite side, so back we went and rowed across, then lay down to them. They were bunched beautifully, about 200. A nasty push against wind and tide; Peter handled the punt grandly. I had my head right down, peering through a coaming alongside the gun. Suddenly "They're in range." I raised my head. I had some sort of fatheaded idea in my mind of them rising simultaneously and cutting a lane through them as they did. But the near fringe started to roll up, looking awfully thin. So, I hesitated... then realising I was likely to be left lamenting, heaved on the string. A lovely roar and the place was littered with wigeon. P. didn't curse me then, there wasn't time and I didn't fully realise what I'd done. For an hour we were incredibly busy, cripple chasing and I was gasping by the end. Two flew and one in the water and we had 41 in the boat. But, if I'd fired when the first bird jumped, P. said we would have had another 15 -20! As it was it was the best shot at wigeon he'd ever made on the Wash. I was midway between the delights of what had happened and the depths of what I might have done.

The rain had eased off now and the tide was rising fast, with a pretty choppy sea. We were still after the last of the cripples when another bunch of wigeon came across and pitched in the sea half a mile behind us, but not liking the feel of the ocean, went ashore almost at once. We got our cripple and rushed to the punt. Peter fairly made her hiss through the water, with the wind and tide now behind us. Again they were nicely bunched -

150 of them and it looked a grand chance. I was praying for a chance to make up for my shortcomings. Then, at about 300 yards the sun came out and changed the world... The wigeon, which had been black, became a mixture of white breasts and red-brown heads. Had we been close enough we must have shown up terribly. P. stopped the punt and held her and then the agony began. There was a tiny cloud moving terribly slowly towards the sun, but the tide was racing up and any minute might float our birds. I don't suppose it was three minutes really until the cloud arrived and it took the sun fairly amidships. And we flew in... "They're coming into range"... slowly raised my head... there was a horrid grating and the boat began to swing off. Just as the first bird sprang I heaved on the lanyard, praying to every god I knew and... "a perfectly timed shot". Lord I was relieved. It was a long shot though and we had a moving half hour collecting cripples. Two got away - both flyers that got up out of range and we had 20 more wigeon aboard.

The sand banks were all covered now and there was no land in sight, only streaks and patches of foam in a grey sea to show where the banks had been. And then the skies opened and rain came in one solid sheet. I must admit I had horrid thoughts of SW gales approaching from the BBC and we were 4 - 5 miles out. There were some patches of sea that seemed to take an awful lot of rowing through, I don't know why. The pump was continually in action. Then we got to the edge of the saltings. It was getting duskish and there were little bunches of wigeon everywhere, mixed up with shelduck, but they wouldn't wait and kept rolling up in front of us all the way home; never thick enough for a shot. Mallard were flighting in early off the sea along with several pintail. There was one big stand of knots quite close to the river, but we were both too weary to be very intrigued, I was anyway.

It was almost like heaven to get into the mouth of the river and be able to paddle quietly up with the tide. We got back to find the lighthouse leaking like a sieve, water everywhere, but we soon puddled that up and put a variety of buckets out to catch the worst of the trickles.

I had to dash off to change and get into Lynn to try to look wise and teach wretched soldiers things that they knew a darn sight more about than I did. How I kept awake I don't know. I certainly couldn't concentrate with pictures of wigeon and grebes and divers and all manner of ducks flying, swimming and running in front of my eyes. But think of the luck of it; my first day and Peter's best on the Wash and within 3 of his best anywhere after wigeon!

The letter then moves on to two or three other dawns and dusks when Nigel was out to the end of that season.

It was on a very hot 2nd August 1937 that the now engaged, Nigel and Corona with their friend John Stephenson spent a few hours shooting at Welney, on the now famous Ouse Washes. They walked from 2.30 to 7.00 pm, had a meal and walked on until dusk. During their tramp across the marshes they collected no less than 36 snipe, 14 mallard, a teal and a gadwall.

By October 1937 the couple had married and there is a splendid little sketch of when, if I remember correctly, they were travelling north on their honeymoon. There is Nigel in a small car which looks like an Austin Seven with a .22 pistol, while Corona, acting as retriever, is climbing over a stone wall with a grouse in hand. From the other direction comes a

134

policeman on a motorcycle. The caption says: Grouse on the
North Road - or -The unexpected speed cop!

Honeymoon 1937 - An unexpected speed-cop

There is so much more but for fear of boring the reader I had
better finish this with one last entry. An episode that I had heard
about. Nigel and Corona with Two others went for a morning
duck flight at Runcton Fen. In the dark Corona took the wrong
gun, leaving Nigel hers, which was far too short in the stock for
him. The bag was 4 mallard, 6 wigeon, 9 teal, 2 pigeon, 2
waterhen, 1 snipe and a rabbit. The accompanying note reads:

*I took N's gun by mistake on getting out of the car - never shot
better and had a grand morning - but N's wrath unprintable as
of course, he nearly broke his thumb every time he fired!*

I was told this story when I stayed with my friends in
Zimbabwe. Corona told it with relish, grinning at Nigel, who
was not really amused even 43 years after the event.

EPILOGUE

Thankfully Nigel was spared the indignity and hurt of being evicted from his farm as it was over a decade after his death that the occupation of white owned farms by the so-called war veterans began. At the age of 90 poor Corona was beaten up and robbed at her house and struggled naked and battered round the dam to get to Richard's house. Amazingly, but to no great surprise to anyone who knows this tough lady, she recovered and told me in one of her subsequent letters, that of the property the thieves took the thing that saddened her most of all was the loss of the little .410 gun that was given to her by her father when she was 14 all those years ago in Norfolk.

I can understand a native people wanting to take back their land which they no doubt look upon as stolen by white colonialists but the majority of the population were just not ready or responsible enough to take on the farms. In any case, who are the rightful owners of Zimbabwe? Probably not the shona and definitely not the matabele who are an off-shoot of the zulu nation. More likely it would the Bushmen or the mysterious ancient peoples who built the stone buildings at Great Zimbabwe.

The current Zimbabwean government would have been far wiser to have continued to work with the white farmers and evolved African farmers to learn to use modern skills to farm the land as a business and not just for their immediate family. In the mean time the country could have fed it's starving neighbours and become a strong and wealthy African state instead of looking for and expecting handouts from the Western world. Now the farms stand idle and thousands of acres of productive land will return to wilderness. Some might say Great. It might be if there were no people to feed – but there are.

The family persuaded Corona to move North to stay with Pip in Mozambique where he had set up a fishing holiday business, hotel-restaurant and cabins combined with a crocodile farm. She made the move and settled but sadly Pip died and although Corona is still in Africa, it is now in a residential home that she lives. The grounds are of an area large enough to harbour a variety of birds including egrets. With failing eyesight this remarkable lady has learned how to use the medium of e-mail to continue her correspondence with her family and friends.

In a recent e-mail she told how the staff of the home had organised a sing-song accompanied by tea, cake and sandwiches. She dryly commented that it was all very nice, but a double whiskey would have gone down well!